Jim Adams

Other Me's

My caregiver experience with Lewy Body Dementia

In memory of
Diane Kay Nelson Adams,
the love of my life.

Dedicated to all those affected by Lewy Body Dementia and the doctors and researchers working to find a cure for this and other mental diseases.

Acknowledgements

Without the support of my family and friends this book would not have been written. They gave me inspiration, guidance, and encouragement to complete this project.

Much gratitude is due my son Greg Adams, English teacher and former newspaper editor, for being my book editor. He kept my engineering style of writing in check and brought forth a story. We have spent many hours editing text and, more importantly, sharing memories of the past few years during his mom's struggle with Lewy Body Dementia. Thanks to his wife Laurie and daughter Addy for giving up their time with Greg so he could edit this project.

Thanks to my daughter Chris Rambo for designing the book cover. In addition to her graphic design talents, Chris has been my "talk to" person in terms of ideas, feelings, and memories. Thanks also go to her husband Mike and children Gwenyth and Reuben for giving up their time with Chris to make this happen.

Special thanks to my son Don Adams for being a solid listener during our regular dinner sessions, and providing rational insight for my projects. Thanks to Heidi, Taylor, and Becca Adams for being an integral part of my life during this difficult time.

Special thanks to friends Kathy Nelson, who lost her spouse to Lewy Body Dementia with Parkinson's Disease, Joanie Lindau, and Linda Dahl, for the many conversations relating to caretaking, grief, and "moving on in life." You reinforced many of the feelings, actions, and reactions I experienced throughout this ordeal. Our "Three Widows and a Widower" talks have been extremely influential in my personal growth while writing this book.

Thanks to the Lake Hallie Memory Care Center in Chippewa Falls, Wisconsin for providing the caretaker notes during my wife's stay there.

Thanks to all the readers who gave me feedback and suggestions to make this project successful.

CONTENTS

Other Me's

My caregiver experience with Lewy Body Dementia

A List of Characters

Diane and Jim Adams: Main characters

Don, Heidi, Taylor, and Becca Adams: Oldest son, daughter- in-law, and grandchildren

Greg, Laurie, and Addy Adams: Middle son, daughter- in-law, and grandchild

Chris, Mike, Gwenyth, and Reuben Rambo: Youngest of Diane and Jim's children, son-in-law, and grandchildren

Norma, Cleo, Roger, Bill, and Mel Nelson: Siblings of Diane Adams

Norman and Thea Nelson: Parents of Diane Adams

Jack and Connie Adams: Twin brother and sister-in-law to Jim Adams

Louise, Mary, and Neil: Friends of Jim and Diane Adams

Cortney, Diana: Hospice nurses

An alarming discovery

There must be fish in that spot, I thought as we slowly motored next to the shoreline. I maneuvered the boat into a small bay where a large, ancient tree had fallen into a patch of lily pads. It was a beautiful early June day in 2013 and Diane, my high school sweetheart and wife of 52 years, was fishing with me. I dropped the anchor, helped Diane get her pole rigged and baited the hook. I settled back to begin fishing myself. I watched her first cast to make sure everything was okay. She raised the rod and thrust it forward. The bait went nowhere. She had forgotten to lift the bail on her reel. Before I could say anything, she immediately tried again with the same results. I reminded her to lift the bail. She didn't know what I was talking about. I pointed out the bail and showed her how to lift it before making a cast. I leaned back to let her try again. She failed. I sidled up next to her and walked through the casting process in steps: get the bait into position at the end of the rod; reach down with the index finger to hold the line; lift the bail on the reel; cast the bait; release the index finger just after reaching the high point of the cast, then crank the reel a turn or two to reset the bail after the bait hits the water.

Diane's high school graduation picture, 1959

As I watched Diane try again and fail in exactly the same way I realized that something was not right. She was concentrating, trying hard to cast correctly. I knew she was having some short-term memory problems and mathematics processing issues, so this didn't seem too extraordinary. I was patient. We tried re-casting many times with the same results.

The next afternoon we went fishing again, this time with a simple, push-button reel for Diane. We found a good place to practice casting, and I explained the process yet again. Diane tried her first cast. She couldn't remember any of the steps. I moved close to her and demonstrated the process, actually holding the rod and reel with her. We did this for three or four casts, and I thought she might be ready to try on her own. I moved out of the way. Diane did crank the bait to a starting position but failed to push the button to hold the bait there. She tried to cast, but of course the bait went nowhere.

I think I worked with Diane for more than an hour, but she could not do this very simple activity. She finally said, "Let's go for a boat ride."

She loved to ride in the boat, watching the shore line and marveling at some of the picturesque lake homes. Once in awhile we would have the pleasure of seeing a bald eagle, an otter family, loons, a kingfisher diving for a minnow, deer and other wildlife along the shore. But this time, I couldn't keep my mind off Diane's inability to cast, something she'd done for decades. We didn't talk about her failure the rest of the day, but I was worried.

Diane at the helm of our boat

This was the first occurrence of Diane's sudden inability to process information and a failure of her mind and hands to accomplish a routine task. I had not observed any such issues in Diane's normal daily

8

activities around the house. She worked in the kitchen with no problems. Working on puzzles, making beds, and house cleaning: these everyday tasks seemed unaffected. Diane would periodically repeat questions, but I didn't think it was serious. It wasn't until I observed a multi-step, brain-and-hands activity like casting a fishing bait that I noticed a disconnect.

When Diane and I eventually discussed her inability to cast, I asked her if she thought it would be a good idea to go to the doctor. She said, "I think I should find out what is going on." That was a great relief to me. I don't know what I would have done if she had refused to go to the doctor. Little did I know we were in for a battle with a mind-and body-destroying illness.

In 2013 this was all new to me, this dysfunction, this disease. This was a world before Robin Williams' death, before his posthumous diagnosis, before I (and most of the world) had even heard of Lewy Body Dementia with Parkinson's Disease.

Realizing things weren't right

Diane always had an excellent memory. She could remember things that I had forgotten long ago. But her memory process was changing. Often during conversations she would stop and try to recall what she was saying or forget the names of people she knew well. Diane was often aware of this and would say things like, "I'm getting old, I guess," or, "My memory isn't what it used to be." But I was getting concerned and suggested that we go see the doctor. She said she wasn't ready for that yet.

Diane on our trip to Washington, DC

Diane was aware that she was having some memory problems. The first incident which made her question whether something was wrong occurred on a bus tour to Washington, D.C., in the spring of 2011. Just as we were returning home, the tour guide announced that we would be in Chetek in about 10 minutes. Diane recalled she had no idea what Chetek looked like or, for that matter, what our house looked like. She said she just couldn't visualize Chetek or our house and was a little frightened about that. Diane never mentioned this incident to me until after we had our first visit to the doctor to check for memory issues.

Another incident, on that same trip, that was unusual and frightening for me happened during a tour bus stop in Iowa. Diane was by my side, and I was pretty involved in looking at some books in the souvenir shop. Returning a book to the shelf, I turned to say something to Diane. She was gone. I searched all over the visitor center for her. I asked the tour director to check the lady's restroom for me, but Diane wasn't there either. I told the tour director I was concerned. "It's not like her to go wander off like that," I explained. I continued to look but could not find my wife. I was very concerned. I checked once more in the lobby of the visitor center, and there she was. I was so happy tears came to my eyes. I walked up to Diane and gave her a big hug. I asked her where she was. "I don't know," she explained, "I just found myself with the tour group, so I stayed with them."

Diane did not recall leaving me in the visitor center or how she got with the group. I remember wanting to scold her, but I was so happy to have her with me it didn't seem proper. While we enjoyed the trip, I was grateful to get home to familiar ground. Home is supposed to be safe, right?

In the spring of 2012 Diane began insisting we keep our doors locked and windows closed, something that was never done on the home farm. She became almost paranoid about this. On hot nights when we left windows open, she would now see people in our backyard when returning to bed after a trip to the bathroom. I would try to catch what she was seeing but would observe nothing except moonlit shadows. Diane saw movement. Diane saw people. I didn't think anything was too abnormal.

Around Christmas of 2012 Diane began asking the same questions repeatedly. I would have to reiterate answers two or three times within a matter of minutes. Our children also began to notice this change in their mom. It was very evident that Diane didn't realize she had just asked the question. Sometimes after I answered a question a time or two she would say, "Oh yes, I just asked that." But that didn't happen very often. Neither of us made much note of this behavior. As a retired high school teacher, I was so used to having to repeat questions and answers for students that it didn't enter my mind that this was unusual behavior for an adult.

In our conversations, the repeating of questions and answers continued but didn't seem to increase. Diane then began to repeat sentences and thoughts, particularly after a small pause in our conversation. These "quiet" periods happened often during our conversations. We are both introverts, and our presence together often meant more to us than words spoken. While it was unusual for Diane to repeat her thoughts after less than a minute's pause in conversation, it didn't seem serious enough to go see a doctor. After all, we were getting older.

In her younger, post-vocational-school days, Diane worked as a bookkeeper and always did the accounting at our house. In the summer and fall of 2013, I began to notice that it was taking her much longer to balance the checkbook. She would also become quite aggravated that the numbers just didn't work out--she was always off by a few pennies. I would help her, and when I added and subtracted the numbers they seemed to work out just fine. As I checked her processes I could see that she would reverse two numbers in the cents column or would forget where she was in the computation process. She would frequently press the wrong keys on her calculator. This was unusual as Diane could previously add, subtract, multiply, or divide numbers without even looking at the keyboard. The speed with which she processed numbers in her head and operated the calculator had deteriorated.

As time went on, the difficulty with number processing seemed to progress rapidly. She would work for several hours at a time, day and evening, over a period of days, wrestling with the figures only to become frustrated. The books wouldn't balance.

It seems strange, but neither of us thought much about these changes. We seemed to sort of pass them off as strange, maybe just part of the aging process. Since the checkbook balancing was done once a month, neither of us thought much about the issue during the other 29 days. It kind of slipped "under the rug" for the rest of the month. If Diane knew of other instances with number problems, she never told me about them. This wouldn't be abnormal. She was so quiet and always had a lot of patience and tenacity when balancing books.

By the winter of 2013 into early 2014, the problems with processing numbers worsened. Diane would now take more than a week to balance the checkbook, and rarely without my assistance. She would have papers strewn about the table in a seemingly random manner. Normally, she would have documents neatly stacked in rows of income and expenses, and within each she would have small groups representing groceries, utilities, insurance, etc. Of course, the "new" lack of organization only contributed to her frustration.

Diane and I would make it a point to walk every day. We had a usual "bark-free" route, as Diane was always a little frightened of strange dogs. We enjoyed the exercise and often had great conversations about our children, grandchildren, our time together, and what we might be doing in the future. The spring of 2013 was different. We were having great conversations, but Diane would physically drift towards or away from me as she walked, not a sudden drift but small direction changes that began to occur regularly. She would tell me it was because of the gradual slope of the road. I passed it off as just that. However, as time went on, I wondered why she would drift away from as well as toward the center where I was walking. It would seem logical to only drift to one side. Here again, we both just laughed it off as "the aging process."

Late in July 2013 after our fishing trip with her brothers Mel and Bill-- the same trip with the casting problems--Diane had a computed tomography (CT) scan of her brain.

We scheduled a doctor's appointment to "find out what was going on." We wanted to see if there was visible damage, possibly a cancerous mass that would cause the symptoms she was experiencing. This wasn't a detailed scan but one to catch any obvious damage or tumor. We always feared that her colon cancer, which she survived in 2003, would return and metastasize to the brain area.

After the CT scan Diane and I sat in the car a while talking about the results, especially the possible recurrence of her cancer. This wasn't easy. Diane's colorectal cancer (removed through surgery but not treated with chemotherapy) had spread to her lungs, forcing a resection operation in 2005. Diane's quality of life had been quite good during her ten-plus years of battling cancer. The only side effect from all her surgeries seemed to be a loss of smell.

13

Only later did we learn that the loss of smell is an early symptom of Lewy Body Dementia with Parkinson's Disease.

Diane told me if the cancer was back, she didn't want any more surgery or treatments. She was tired of being tested and poked with needles, knowing that the cancer would likely return. We had both outlived our parents and agreed that we had lived wonderful lives. If God wanted to take us, he could do so any time that was right for Him. This conversation was an incredible help to me as Diane progressed through her end of life experience.

Journaling to "find the right words"

Diane was seeing a speech therapist to help with "finding the right words" when she tried to remember things. One suggested activity was to start a daily journal. This is something Diane had never done, nor had I. I thought it was a good idea as it would help her recall what had happened each day and work her hand, brain, and eye coordination. To set a good example, I decided to keep a journal along with Diane; that way, we could spend time together writing our entries each day.

What you read from this point on are my journal entries from September 11, 2013, until October 5, 2014, the day after our celebration of life for Diane. It is a 445-day chronicle of events describing the progression of dementia, the stark difference between my life as a caregiver and Diane's life experiencing the loss of brain and bodily function, and what caretakers at Diane's memory care center experienced on a daily basis.

To distinguish between the various perspectives of this journey, I have used the following fonts to differentiate points of view:

Emboldened and italicized--daily entries to my personal journal.

Italicized--entries made by the caregivers at the memory care center (as they appeared in the daily notes).

Regular--my post-experience reflections; family members' reactions and reflections also use this font.

-- Wednesday, September 11, 2013 --

Diane called me in the middle of a model airplane club meeting wondering where the kids were. She was sure we had to take care of the kids. I just explained that the kids were at their homes, and it was just the two of us living at our house.

We are going down to visit Chris, Mike, Gwen, and Reuben tomorrow.

"The kids" that Diane was concerned about are our grandchildren (in this case, Gwen and Reuben). At this early stage of dementia it was easy to convince her that everything was okay. I could just tell her, "The kids are at their homes. It's just the two of us in our house."

-- Thursday, September 12, 2013 --

Diane and I stayed with Gwenyth and Reuben while Chris did some shopping. Chris returned after a couple of hours and got both kids to sleep as only a mom can do.

Chris and Mike have a two-story house, and Diane could no longer carry the grandchildren up the stairs due to her balance problems. In fact, she couldn't get out of a chair if she was holding the baby. She loved to feed little Reuben his bottle. When she was finished, I would take Reuben from her and place him in his playpen or on the floor to play.

I'm sitting at our kitchen table writing with Diane, trying to help her remember some of the day's events. It is very difficult for her to remember the time, day, and recall any details of what happened.

Helping Diane remember daily events was like teaching students with learning difficulties. It required me to search for prompts, usually a person, an event, or a visual scene, that might cause a jog in her memory. To sit with her at our kitchen table and realize her memory was slowly slipping away was a dreadful thought. I often had to hold back tears as I watched her struggle to remember and force a simple sentence on to her journal page. The thought "Alzheimer's Disease" was constantly with me.

We both fell asleep in front of the TV after we came back. Diane thought our granddaughter Addy was staying at our house tonight. This is common when she wakes up from an afternoon's sleep. She often thinks the kids are here or are missing from the house.

-- Friday, September 13, 2013--

We had an 11 AM appointment in Rice Lake with the speech therapist. The appointment went well. Heidi, the therapist, was pleased with

16

Diane's notes and activities. We have been trying to get Diane to organize and write her daily activities just to get her to do more hand/mind activities. It is still very difficult to get Diane to write. We'll have to get a jigsaw puzzle going so there is at least some problem-solving activity.

Diane did kitchen work and has been trying to understand a billing from the clinic concerning the brain scan that was done in July 2013. I don't even understand the "billing," so it must be very confusing for Diane.

Diane would have papers laid out all over our kitchen table trying to make sense of the bills. The fact that she could no longer do our household bookkeeping didn't seem to prevent her from trying to understand the medical billing system. I often think about how frustrating it must have been for Diane to see all the numbers and codes and not be able to process them in a sensible manner. I must admit, I have extreme difficulty understanding medical billing and often can't understand or make logical sense of them either.

-- Saturday, September 14, 2013 --

Diane put a roast in the crock pot and had no problems using a recipe from a cookbook. She also washed clothes. The washing machine had a problem getting stuck on the agitate cycle. I started it over on a new wash cycle, and that seemed to fix the problem for now.

Diane started having problems with the washing machine quite often. I used my computer to make a large print, step-by-step procedure for her and taped it to the lid of the washing machine. This seemed to help her remember how to start the washing machine.

-- Sunday, September 15, 2013 --

Diane had dreams and hallucinations last night. Animals were coming in the house and getting food. She wasn't afraid of the animals but said the hallucination lasted longer than usual.

I would ask Diane to tell me details about her dreams. What kind of animals were they? Where did the animals go in the house to find food? Were the animals scary? How many were there? Often she couldn't identify the animals; they were just animals. The animals would come in the house through windows, under doors, and sometimes just "appear." Periodically, the animals would open the doors in the cupboards to find food.

After dinner I helped Diane with her stretch exercises using the elastic band tied to the door knob. She did very well.

Diane didn't have difficulty doing the exercises prescribed by the physical therapist. The difficulty was reading the instructions and remembering which exercises she had completed. I would read the directions and show her how to do the exercises and complete them along with her. For any involving balance, I would stand by her just in case she was about to fall.

-- Monday, September 16, 2013 --

Diane and I went for a walk taking the long route. I did my usual exercises this morning also.

I practiced banjo for a while in the afternoon. I'm finally getting the vamping down so I can chord quite well with some simple bluegrass tunes. I love this instrument.

I worked on the landing gear on the Taylorcraft again and tweaked the angles of the wheels. I'm ready to practice welding on the 5/32 inch landing gear wire.

Quarter scale model of the Taylorcraft

My hobbies helped me deal with the stress I felt as Diane's health declined and my caretaker responsibilities increased. Building a scale model airplane involves continuous engineering and problem solving, which gave me relief from the worry and stress over Diane's condition. Playing guitar, harmonica, and banjo did the same thing. When I'm playing an instrument, my hands and mind are fully involved, providing temporary relief of worry and stress.

-- Tuesday, September 17, 2013 --

Banjo lesson day! Yes!

I slept in a little late this morning because Diane and I talked until 11:30 last night. We talked about finding a hobby that she might enjoy. We're still thinking about it. If we could just find something that would keep her hands and mind more active...

Finding Diane a hobby had been a struggle from the time we were married. We tried everything from ceramics to scrapbooking. The only thing she persisted with was putting jigsaw puzzles together. She would spend hours doing this and really enjoyed the satisfaction of completing a large and difficult puzzle. We never found anything else she enjoyed enough to keep pursuing. I have so many hobbies, perhaps too many, but I could never get Diane interested in anything other than putting puzzles together. I often wonder if she had had a hobby such as woodworking or indoor/outdoor gardening if that would have helped delay dementia.

We went for a walk using the long route but on the other side of HWY SS past the elementary school. There were lots of dogs barking at us on this route.

I talked with Neil a little before going to my banjo lesson.

Neil is a very good friend of mine. He is a commercial pilot who, until recently, flew charter jets all over the world. We have similar interests from engineering to model building. I can't express how important it is to have a friend like Neil while going through a battle with dementia. I could share what I was experiencing as a caregiver. We have had many hours of very personal conversations, I think to the benefit of us both.

-- Wednesday, September 18, 2013 --

At the doctor's office we waited for more than an hour. Diane had "improved" on her tests since last month. They want Diane to do more socializing, and we sure started that out today!

Diane and I were taken by surprise when two of the guys I fly model airplanes with came over in the evening about 6:30 PM. Luckily, we had cleaned the house and baked a cake. I had written the meeting down in the Thursday calendar box because Wednesday's was filled up with appointments. I forgot to draw an arrow to Wednesday's box. So--surprise!

20

Diane did great. She listened and watched what we were doing on the computer, which I had connected to our TV. Diane frosted the cake and Neil's wife Annette helped her serve cake and drinks to everyone. We had a great meeting, but I was in the dog house for sure!

-- Thursday, September 19, 2013 --

I counted Diane's pills out last evening to increase her depression meds from 150 mg to 200 mg. Well, I checked this afternoon, and she had taken all the pills out and gotten confused trying to get the 200 mg right. I have to watch this for sure! Diane does well with daily tasks, but there are problems with dates, times, and mathematics.

Diane battled depression for many years. It was well controlled with the medication she was taking, and I could definitely tell when she didn't take her medication. If she failed to take the medicine, she would easily become teary-eyed over little things that didn't seem to go right for her. She would also become worried about small things that seemed unimportant. I didn't like to see her in this state. It was very important to keep her on schedule with her medications. Dementia combined with depression is a treacherous mix.

-- Friday, September 20, 2013 --

We visited the speech therapist at 11 AM. Diane is struggling with writing and organization. I'm not sure if the act of journaling and trying to organize thoughts is helping Diane or making her more frustrated. I know these activities are good for brain cell activity.

Last evening, as I was reading, Diane came in from the kitchen asking if her sister Cleo was here. She said she thought she heard Cleo talking. Diane also asked if anyone was staying here tonight.

Cleo was the nearest sister to Diane in terms of age and was a super role model for Diane. This is not to imply Diane wasn't close to her other siblings. In fact, the siblings are very close to each other to this day. This is the family I was so lucky to have married into.

Hearing Cleo talking was the first time that auditory hallucinations had come into play. Diane was so sure that Cleo was there that she heard her talking. She heard Cleo while in the kitchen, and the sound must have appeared to come from where I was in the living room. These hallucinations were so real to Diane it made me wonder about reality.

I continually have to explain to Diane why she is writing things down. It's hard for her to understand why she should be doing something she has never had to do before.

Getting out and about

-- Saturday, September 21, 2013 --

After playing music at the Touched Twice mission event, Diane and I went to Laurie's parents' 45th wedding anniversary celebration at the nursing home in Fall Creek, Wisconsin, where Laurie's mother Dori is a resident.

Diane did well at the anniversary party. She talked with people, fed little Reuben, and ate some of the excellent food, something I was happy to see since she hasn't had much of an appetite the last couple of months.

Diane, like me, has always been very introverted. We both gain our strength from being alone with our thoughts. Sometimes we wouldn't say anything to each other for hours while sitting home alone in the evening. Simply being together was the most reassuring thing to both of us. With the advent of her dementia, Diane became much more sensitive to crowds and didn't enjoy being around a lot of people. She stayed very close to me, and I certainly didn't mind that. Whenever we were out in public, I would make sure I always had her in my vision and stayed alert to her facial and body language, just in case she became afraid or needed help.

-- Monday, September 23, 2013 --

Diane and I went down to Chris and Mike's to be with the little ones while Mike and Chris were out. It is so precious to be able to hold Gwen and read to her and rock with her. Little Reuben napped for a little while then woke up and rocked with Diane for a time. They are growing so fast.

Last night Diane was quite tired and was confused about where Don, Greg, and Chrissy were. As I was about to go to bed she was in the hall coming out to see who was in the house. I explained that the kids were all at their own houses--then she remembered. Tiredness seems to make her dementia worse.

It is interesting that in the confusion of dementia, Diane saw our children at different ages and stages in life. This particular time they were all at home but at their younger high school or middle school age. It was like each of them was off somewhere and expected to return or call to let Diane know how things were going. Very often Diane would walk into a room and wonder where everyone was, as if she expected other people in the house.

-- Tuesday, September 24, 2013 --

Diane washed some clothes and has been working on a puzzle most of the afternoon. She still asks about whether or not the kids are home from school. She knows she keeps asking these things but doesn't know why. Well, neither do I.

-- Wednesday, September 25, 2013 --

Diane and I went for a walk about 2 PM. We took the long route. About the time we got to our son Greg's, about halfway through the walk, Diane began to walk faster than normal, as if she were driven by something. She seemed to lean forward as she walked. As we approached our house she was sweating and obviously tired. I opened the front door and turned around to see Diane reaching her hand to me. I took her hand, and she kneeled down on the floor. I told her to lay down and rest on the floor while I got a cool cloth for her head. After about 10 minutes she got up by herself and sat in the chair. I think we might do shorter, more frequent walks rather than the long route. VERY SCARY!

This was a completely new turn of events. I remember telling Diane to slow down as we got closer to the house. I could tell she was warm, as her face was flushed. She didn't seem to pay attention to me. She just kept up the fast, forward-leaning pace. After she recovered, I asked if she remembered what had happened. She said, "I felt like I was floating."

-- Thursday, September 26, 2013 --

We are writing in our journals. It's about 4:30 PM. Diane is struggling to remember anything to write. If I prompt her it helps. Right now she is having problems writing "2013." She started with "20014" then "20013" and then after I prompted her she wrote "2013."

It was painful to see how Diane's writing was degrading. Not only was writing numbers difficult, but her handwriting itself was becoming hard to read. Diane's handwriting was always very neat and proper, much better than mine ever was. Now there was a waviness to the characters, and the spacing between letters and words was uneven. Watching this was frustrating and extremely sad, like seeing a student continue to get worse after spending countless hours practicing to master a skill. It's the direct opposite of what I was able to see in the students I taught.

-- Friday, September 27, 2013 --

We had our last speech therapy session today. Diane did really well. She talked and read from her journal more than she had in the past. We all think boosting the dosage of meds is helping. The therapists were very pleased with Diane's progress.

-- Saturday, September 28, 2013 --

Today Diane was wondering if her mom was here. After a short while, Diane realized her mom was gone. She still asks about Cleo and our kids being in the house.

This week Diane has been much better in terms of being more alert. She called her sister Norma last night and Cleo tonight. It is really good for her to talk to other people.

-- Monday, September 30, 2013 --

I did my normal exercises. Diane got up early today at 7:30 AM. I practiced banjo while she was getting ready for the day.

We have Bible study at our house one week from today, so Diane is starting the house cleaning ritual.

This house cleaning behavior was totally normal, and totally welcomed. Not only did it reflect a bit of Diane's old routine, it gave her a chance to use her hands and mind in an activity that she was used to. I tried to let her do everything by herself, but sometimes she would ask me to help reach something or lift something that might require some balance. For the most part, she handled the cleaning tasks very well. Diane did drop a small object off a shelf while dusting, but nothing I couldn't fix.

-- Tuesday, October 1, 2013 --

As we were at the table eating lunch, Diane began seeing other people sitting in the kitchen chair. This happened twice. One person was our speech therapist. There was also a kid with his mom...and something to do with insurance.

When Diane saw others at the table, she would look at me, lower her voice to a whisper, and ask if I could see what she was seeing. My first inclination was to tell her that I could see the people also. However, the hallucination would often fade before I could answer. She would just say, "He's gone," and that was it. I would almost always ask her who the people were to try to understand what was going on in her mind. Sometimes she could identify who she was seeing; other times, she didn't know who it was.

The insurance connection was easy for me to understand. Diane worked at an insurance agency after we moved to California to support me through college. Diane worked full time, and I went to aeronautical engineering school full time. She worked at the agency the entire two and a half years it took for me to graduate. I always told her she had her PHT degree: "Putting Hubby Through." Connections with insurance within her mind were certainly there, and now the brain was traversing paths from the past and making almost random connections to other stored information.

-- Wednesday, October 2, 2013 --

Diane is regularly having visions of our kids being in the house. She is also confused about having to move from our house. She couldn't understand how we got all "this stuff" in this house so quickly. Just before going to bed she came out to the living room wondering where the kids were. She insisted that Greg was sitting on the couch while we were eating, along with an unidentified friend of Don's.

This was the first evidence of Capgras Syndrome--a condition that causes the brain to see a person as several different people, and places change from one place to another, in an instant--although we didn't know it at the time.

What happened here is amazing to me. How the brain can scramble connections in this manner is baffling. Diane would be sitting with me in our living room while we were reading or watching TV and ask, "When did we move to this house?" She couldn't understand how all our household goods were instantaneously moved to this house, as if we had an identical house in some other virtual world. Not only that, but all our belongings could be suddenly moved from one house to the other. I didn't know how to react to this strange development. Seeing other people and hearing voices was one thing, but two identical houses with instant transfer of belongings, that was something completely different!

Weird confusion

-- Thursday, October 3, 2013 --

About 4 AM Diane got up and walked to the hall, turned around and came back. I asked if she was OK. She said, "I have to get out of here." To her, we were in some place in the Twin Cities and had to leave because of "sex." I convinced her we were at our house.

The word "sex" was unusual in Diane's conversation. In her family sex was seldom mentioned. Her parents were very strict about the subject. We never had problems talking about sex in our relationship, but Diane was very uncomfortable when there were sexy scenes in a movie or when others would talk about anything in a sexual manner. It was important that I tell her, "Yes, we are getting out of here." I then could help her understand that she had a "dream." We were at our house and things were okay.

We are going to a friend's funeral this morning. She had cancer and was very sick for a long time.

Diane was very confused in the late afternoon and evening. We just talked for an hour. She was thinking that we had our house taken by some officials and were living in a different house. She couldn't understand how we got all our stuff moved so quickly. She was still confused about the "dream" she had last night. In that incident, we were down south in Alabama where someone forced me to smoke something. The conversation was quite incoherent.

According to Diane, one of the reasons for having to move to another house was that our current house was being confiscated by officials. This scenario would prove to be quite dominant as time went on. When Diane talked about the "dream," it happened in Alabama this time, not in the Twin Cities, and "sex" had been replaced with smoking something.

These conversations would last an hour, sometimes longer. It is extremely difficult to try to determine what kind of a thought path Diane's brain was on. I was usually able to make some sort of connection, be it ever so small, that would help make sense of Diane's thought process at the time. This way I could hold a somewhat meaningful conversation with her.

-- Friday, October 4, 2013 --

I finished vacuuming the house while Diane was getting ready, as she slept until 10 AM this morning. She said she slept well because we were "back here."

Diane is having problems keeping track of the number of pills she should take. I have put the correct number of pills in the daily portion box, but each evening she dumps them out and recounts them, often getting them mixed up. I'll probably go to a single portion in a paper cup and put the med bottles where she can't get at them.

I brought the church newsletter up on the computer downstairs so Diane could read it. When she came down the stairs she saw two people, "A man and a woman, nicely dressed like they had good jobs," sitting in the room. She didn't know them, but Diane felt they were members of the group who took our house and is gathering information on us.

This idea of someone gathering information on us was new but would play a repeating role as time went on.

-- Saturday, October 5, 2013 --

I was reading my devotions around 7 AM this morning and heard Diane in the hall. I was sitting in the kitchen/den area with the kitchen light on. She wanted to know what was going on. I told her, "Nothing. Why?" Diane said I was acting strange. I wasn't my usual self. I seemed different. I explained that I wasn't different in any way, but that didn't satisfy her. She just said, "OK," and went back to bed.

This was the first time that Diane saw me differently. She couldn't express what made me different, but something about me wasn't the same. This puzzled me a lot. There was no history of my acting differently throughout our marriage, so it wasn't like the case of insurance where there was a history of connections. This phenomenon would become a large part of the Capgras Syndrome later in this journey.

-- Monday, October 7, 2013 --

It's Diane's birthday today. We are both 72 years old now. Today Norma, Cleo, and Mel came up to celebrate the day. We visited a while, played lots of music, and then had cake and ice cream.

-- Tuesday, October 8, 2013 --

Diane is still confused towards the end of the day, particularly wondering where the kids are. She was wondering where Cleo and Mel were. They were here yesterday.

-- Wednesday, October 9, 2013 --

Almost all day today, Diane kept wondering where the grandkids were. I keep saying to her, "It's just you and me, Hon." She has a hard time understanding why she gets so confused. SO DO I!

A frustrating aspect of this stage was Diane's periodic cognizance that there was something wrong. She knew she was confused but had no comprehension of why. We talked several times about dementia and how it affects people's thinking, but that part of the conversation didn't seem to stick. Throughout the day I tried my best to explain why she got so confused--her illness, her dementia--but I was never successful.

-- Thursday, October 10, 2013 --

Diane is having major difficulty figuring out when her haircut is. Dates and days are major hurdles. It has taken about 40 minutes for her to study the calendar and dates. She finally told me to make sure I remind her and get her up early so she gets to the appointment on time.

During this 40-minute period, Diane stood by the wall calendar with a pencil and paper. She would point to and count the day boxes, write something down on her paper, then go back and count the day boxes again. She would erase what she had written the first time and then write something down again. Diane would repeatedly ask me what day it was. In total exasperation she would gently fold up the paper and put it in the garbage.

I had a good banjo practice in the evening. I'm doing a lot of repetitive chord changes and picking exercises. It must be hard for Diane to listen to, but she never complains.

-- Saturday, October 12, 2013 --

Our model airplane club has our last fun fly of the year today. We have a bonfire at the end of the day using all the crashed model airplanes from the season, as well as hamburgers on the grill.

I came home about the time it was getting dark. Diane was very worried about what had happened to Greg. He was here and left without her knowing it. Greg hasn't been here since morning.

After being gone for this model airplane club meeting, I began to think that leaving Diane alone at the house might not be a good idea. I had thoughts of her leaving the house, in this case, looking for Greg. She may not have remembered that Greg and Laurie's house is just a block down the street. The thought of Diane ending up lost devastated me. My son Greg told me of his experience with his neighbor lady who had dementia. He spotted her wandering almost a mile from her house as he was driving through town. He picked her up and drove her back home. I couldn't bear the thought of that happening with Diane.

-- Sunday, October 13, 2013 --

Diane slept during the entire Green Bay football game. She was really tired.

I practiced banjo for about 45 minutes and went to bed just after the news on TV. I had just gotten into bed when Diane came in wondering what was going on. She thought we were taking care of a little girl, though she didn't know who the girl was. I just explained that we were alone, and there was no little girl to worry about. "How do you know all these things?" she often asks.

Granddaughter Addy was "our little girl," as we cared for her daily from the time she was born until she began attending school. It's no surprise that Diane would be concerned about a little girl. Diane was always a caring, loving, person. She cared not who "the little girl" was; what mattered was that "the little girl" was cared for. This worry over a "little girl" continued throughout her battle with dementia.

-- Monday, October 14, 2013 --

We had a pretty busy schedule today. The first thing is to get the boat ready for winter storage: done.

The second task was to seal the basement window where water had leaked in during some heavy rain.

The third task was to remove the small air conditioner from the master bedroom. Diane and I moved it with no problems.

The fourth task was to go grocery shopping--UGH!

At this stage in her dementia, Diane was able to help me with most household tasks. She seemed to enjoy helping around the house. As long as I was there to help her remember what had to be done next things were okay.

-- Thursday, October 17, 2013 --

Diane was unhappy tonight that the kids were not here--she wondered if she "counted" anymore. This breaks my heart!

When Diane, whom I loved very much, wondered if she "counted" anymore, it was like someone knocking the wind out of me. I remember holding her and telling her she counted a lot with me and always will. It was incredibly difficult at times like this to remember, "It is not Diane, it is the dementia." I can't recall a time in our lives when Diane felt like she didn't count. She was always important to me and our children. We couldn't get along without her.

-- Friday, October 18, 2013 --

Diane asked if I had seen her dad then realized he had passed away years ago. She also asked if we were getting a divorce. She was very concerned about this. I explained that wouldn't happen. It was just her mind playing tricks on her. She is also confused about where we are and often asks if we are going "home."

Often Diane would realize she had said or asked something that didn't make sense, like wondering if I had seen her deceased father. She would correct herself and shake her head in disbelief.

Asking me if we were getting a divorce was another jolt, particularly after she wondered if she "counted" anymore. Such a statement, even coming from the dementia, struck deep into my being. I explained to her I would never divorce her, that I loved her very much, and that her mind was playing tricks on her. She seemed to accept that.

-- Saturday, October 19, 2013 --

I'm headed to church at 10:30 to serve potatoes at the Lutefisk dinner. Diane will come down at 1:30, and we'll finish around 3 PM.

Diane didn't come down at 1:30. I called to see if she was coming. She said she would come if I could tell her where to turn. I just told her to stay there, and I would be home in a little while.

Our church is two blocks straight east of our house. We have driven and walked there countless times. In this instance, Diane hadn't realized what the time was, and she didn't know how to get to the church. When I got home I gave her a hug and told her she didn't have to go to the church that afternoon.

I was quickly realizing things were progressing quite rapidly in the wrong direction for Diane. I had signed up for a Powerful Tools for Caregivers class from our county's Office Of Aging, which is part of the Aging and Disability Resource Center in Barron, Wisconsin. My thought was, "I have a lot to learn and need to start soon."

Getting external help

-- Monday, October 21, 2013 --

I wrote a letter to Diane's doctor today describing the progression of dementia and the speed with which it seems to be moving. I think the information will help with our next appointment.

I got a phone call from the Barron County Office on Aging letting me know about the caregiver class I signed up for. It was starting on Wednesday at noon in Rice Lake. I'll be attending once a week for six weeks.

The timing of this phone call couldn't have been better. I knew I needed some help with caregiving. I also wanted to know what other people in my situation were doing that would help me better care for Diane.

I emailed the letter I wrote to our doctor to each of our children. The children did indeed call Diane often just to talk and let her know they are all right, as requested in the letter.

Update on Diane Adams (b. 10/7/1941) – sent to children Friday Oct. 18, 2013:

The dementia is progressing at what seems to be a rather rapid rate. Here are some of the things that are happening:

> There is confusion about where we are living. For Mom, we are being threatened by someone (unknown) who is trying to take our house from us. Sometimes we live down south, like Alabama. Sometimes she doesn't know where we are and wonders how "they" got everything in the house and made it look just like our house looks now.

> There is daily concern about "the kids" and wondering where they are. I think she believes you are all in high school yet. She

regularly asks where Greg, or Don, or Chris is and often "sees" you here in the house and leaving the house to go somewhere.

Today, October 18, 2013, while we were baking pies, she asked if I had seen her dad. She realized before I could answer that he had passed away years ago. She also asked if everyone knew about our separation and getting a divorce. I told her that was never going to happen, but I don't really know if she believes me.

Mom asked me if I talked to the ghosts. She said she sometimes sees them but doesn't understand why I can't see them. She regularly sees people in our house and often wants to know what happened to them and where they went.

Yesterday she wondered where the kids were and why they never come back to the house. Mom made the statement, "Don't I count anymore?" Breaks my heart.

She wonders how long a trip it is to the church and how long it will take to get back. (We are two blocks away.)

I don't think she could, at this point, handle making a pie or cake on her own. It takes a long time–like minutes--to try to figure out what should be done next.

I chopped up a bunch of carrots for soup yesterday. When I got ready to put them in the soup, I discovered she had scraped them into the garbage. Also, there are always things misplaced and lost, particularly parts to things like the blender.

Mom knows there is a problem with her thought processes but can't understand what is causing all this–wish we all could answer that one.

So, I'm thinking that it might be a good idea if each of you could call Mom regularly on her cell phone, even if it's only a minute just to let her know she "counts" and that you are all OK. I think we will also try to have some short visits–we'll come down for an hour just to let her see where you are and that things are just fine. We'll have to work this out with everyone. It's good for her to talk with others.

Jim Adams

-- Tuesday, October 22, 2013 --

Diane wants to start getting up earlier, around 7:30 AM. I think this would be better for her than getting up at 9:30. We often don't eat breakfast because it is too close to noon lunch. I hope that will work.

I went in to wake Diane. She wanted to know what time we had to leave. I told her we were not going anywhere today. She said, "I'll sleep a little longer." I'll try again at 8:00 AM.

Diane and I watched a movie tonight. It was interesting because she had to keep up with reading subtitles since most of the spoken parts were in French. Diane said she didn't follow all the movie due to the subtitles. Lesson learned!

We didn't come close to finishing the movie. I could see that Diane was having problems understanding what was happening. There were several characters to remember, scenes changed rapidly, and she had to try and comprehend the plot by reading the English subtitles. I should have turned the movie off in the first few minutes. At this point I had a lot to learn about dealing with dementia.

-- Wednesday, October 23, 2013 --

I did my exercises and woke Diane up at 8:00 AM.

She wanted to make sure I was in the house and the doors were locked while she was showering and getting ready for the day.

Diane's paranoia was getting worse. Her concern over locked doors and windows had turned to people, specifically other kids, "Boy Scouts," and adults. She was suspicious of these people entering her bedroom at night, seeing her while dressing, or being near the bathroom when she

37

was showering and getting ready for the day. At this point in time it seemed she was okay as long as I was in the house.

The doctor's assistant called while I was on my way to class in Rice Lake. We set up an appointment for Diane at 3 PM on Friday. They feel the rapid progression of Diane's dementia is unusual and they want to see her. This is probably the result of the letter I sent them on Monday.

I arrived at Bethany Lutheran Church. Chris, one of the facilitators for the caregiver class, is a former graduate student of mine. She graduated from the second Barron learning community in 2002. It was good to see her, and she did an excellent job of co-facilitating the class.

The class focused as much on taking care of ourselves as the caregiving process itself. That makes sense. I got a book on caring for Alzheimer's dementia. We had to make an action plan to do something for ourselves each day and follow that plan during the next week.

Prior to attending this first session of the caregiver class, I had never thought about myself and the importance of taking good care of myself. I could not be a good caregiver if I didn't take care of myself. I must admit this wasn't as easy as it sounds.

I wanted to be the best caregiver possible for Diane. She came first in my mind. I had my hobbies to help relieve my anxiety over the dementia, but I didn't set aside regular times or consider other methods of relief such as reading humor or watching old TV programs that would make me laugh. I needed to change my own behavior so I could ultimately become a better caregiver to Diane.

-- Thursday, October 24, 2013 --

I went to wake Diane up and found her door shut, light on in the bedroom. Upon opening the door, I found her sitting on the chair. She said she didn't know what to do and was afraid if she went to take a shower some of the kids (Boy Scouts) would come in the bathroom.

I could relate to Diane's brain latching onto Boy Scouts. My brother Jack and I were counselors at Camp Decorah, a Scout camp near La Crosse, Wisconsin during summers while in high school. Diane had visited the camp several times. Our boys were involved in Boy Scouts and Cub Scouts, and Diane had been a den mother.

I had also worked with kids in other ways over the years. After we moved to Chetek, Wisconsin, we had Bible studies for high school kids in our home on a regular basis. Diane never seemed to mind these activities but her dementia has certainly created much paranoia involving youth in the house.

There is a lot of confusion for Diane today. We've been talking all day about "the other house" and the legal paperwork. I try to change the subject, but that doesn't help. Diane has two watches on her wrist because "The band on one is too large." She was putting towels back in the closet this morning and turned to me and said, "I've made up my mind. I'm staying here." We both agreed to stay in this house. However, there is still much worry and confusion about legal papers for taxes.

When we moved from Colorado to Wisconsin in 1978, it was obvious we couldn't make it financially on my teacher's wages alone. Diane, previously a stay-at-home mom, went to work for a local law office where she often took care of the paperwork for real estate transactions. Her understanding of the terms, documents, and signature requirements was excellent. All this knowledge was stored in her brain, but her dementia was causing her to make connections that were illogical, unrelated, repetitive, and, to her, worrisome.

Paranoia over the proper wording and signatures on the legal papers for our house, and delusions of people scheming to take away our house, became very prevalent. Diane worried about possible liens against the house that needed to be taken care of. She would want to see the satisfaction of deed for the house to confirm there were no liens listed. This became very confusing because she was convinced we had two houses: "the other house" and "this house." I always had to ask questions to try to figure out which house she was thinking about at any given time.

Often the entire day would revolve around legal paperwork for the house and taxes. There were endless questions about tax preparation, if certain deductions were taken, or if there was a canceled check to show payment to a charity. Sometimes the questions made sense, but I had given the same answers over and over. I remember feeling more mentally drained from days like this than from coming home after a day of teaching high school.

-- Friday, October 25, 2013 --

We had a 3PM appointment with our doctor's assistant who asked many questions. Diane went through a blood test, chest x-ray, and urine test. All came back okay. It appears that there is no infection causing Diane's condition. Diane did better on her depression quiz and quite well on the memory test.

We are going to get a brain MRI with enough detail to see if there is any brain damage or degradation. This will usually show any Alzheimer's damage or shrinkage in areas of the brain caused by other conditions.

Diane didn't want to have any more tests, especially after her cancer experience, but said she would do the MRI if it would help us understand what was happening to her. I was thankful for her agreeing to do this, as I wanted to understand what was happening, what we were ultimately dealing with.

The doctor's assistant mentioned Parkinson's Disease because of a few factors: Diane's left arm wasn't swinging when she walked, she leaned forward with no arm movement at the end of longer walks, had a slight tremor in the lips, and experienced balance issues.

We are going to try a new drug to see if it will help with Diane's hallucinations.

I was a little concerned about antipsychotic drugs due to my research into Alzheimer's Disease. Clinicians have to be extremely careful, as some drugs might make symptoms worse and even cause early death in patients. Risperidone was one of those drugs; however, the doctor had to start somewhere and see what the effects were.

The Risperidone experiment

-- Saturday, October 26, 2013 --

Diane took her first Risperidone.

Greg, Laurie, and Addy are coming for a pizza/movie party this afternoon/evening. We're looking forward to that.

I also practiced banjo from 11 AM to noon to keep with my caretakers goal for the week and read chapter 1 of the Caregivers Handbook.

We had pizza with Greg, Laurie and Addy and played Yahtzee while Diane put things away in the kitchen. Diane didn't want to play. She was really confused after everyone left.

At the end of this day there didn't seem to be any visible signs that the Risperidone was causing any significant side effects.

-- Sunday, October 27, 2013 --

Diane and I went down to Eau Claire to have brunch with Mike, Chris and the kids. Diane is confused about where she is and where we are going. She's thinking that we have to take something or pick up "the kids."

Diane has been confused all day--almost constant concern about our house, packing suitcases, meetings, not telling the difference between today and Halloween (which is Thursday), wondering about some committee I'm supposed be involved in.

Things are progressing rapidly in the wrong direction. We'll see how the new medicine will work.

8:20 PM: Diane is totally lost and irrational. I went downstairs to use the bathroom and came up, not seeing Diane anywhere. She was talking to someone in the kitchen dinette area. I asked who she was talking to (it was the coat rack), and she said her friend. She looked at the coat rack and asked her friend how she was doing. Her friend was cold. Diane told her friend she had to go to the bathroom now, and she did. Diane has been seeing "people" all evening, and there is no rational thoughts being expressed.

I went to the kitchen during the Packers game to get an apple. Diane was standing next to the coat rack again. I asked her if she wanted an apple. She said, "No thanks, but my friend might." She talked to the "friend" and put an apple in my coat pocket (hanging on the coat rack). Diane gave the coat rack a hug and a kiss and told her "friend" she had to go to the bathroom. UGH!

It took a day and a half, but the side effects of the Risperidone hit with a vengeance, suddenly and severely. I had never seen Diane so irrational. She was having audio as well as visual hallucinations. She was very agitated, meandering aimlessly through the house. She seemed to be "spaced out," looking off into the distance as she moved and talking with "people" she was seeing. I was frightened.

-- Monday, October 28, 2013 --

We had a very rough night/morning. Diane woke up at around 4:30 AM, seeing Reuben on the bed and concerned with him falling off. She has been completely irrational. I recorded some of our conversations. She regularly sees people outside and inside the house. She saw blue trees, water in the front yard with ducks, people on a motorcycle with their friends inside the house. She regularly talks to those she sees.

Yesterday, last night and today showed marked increases in mental instability, hallucinations, and irrationality.

I don't know if it is the Risperidone or if all this is from the Setraline (anti-depressant) dosage increase.

It must have been the Risperidone, and it had to stop. We had found a drug that made things worse, just as the articles warned. But I could not blame the doctor. There is no test to see how a particular patient reacts to a certain drug. We had to start somewhere. Risperidone was not a good start for Diane.

I called our physician's assistant and told her of the increased symptoms.

We went down to Greg's house to fix a light switch. Diane thought we were at the church.

This afternoon Diane has been playing in Chris's old room talking to little ones. She was trying to put a little sleeper on a child but the child disappeared.

Both our daughter Chris and granddaughter Addy used the bedroom mentioned above. That's where Chris's daughter Gwenyth heads when she visits us, to find the toys. While reacting to the Risperidone, Diane used doll blankets to act out her hallucinations. She would tightly roll up a small blanket. That was the baby. She then wrapped this roll with another blanket as if it were a child and carried it around the house for a long time. She even wanted me to take a picture of her with the baby.

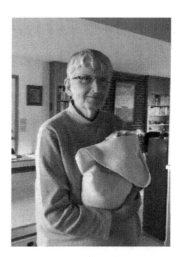

Diane's picture with her "baby"

Our doctor's assistant called, and we are stopping the Risperidone. I had already stopped giving Diane the drug. We are going to try

*another medicine that is used in the treatment of Parkinson's. We will
be scheduling the MRI also.*

*Diane finally went to bed at about 11:30 PM after spending a hour or
so tending "a little one" in Chris's old room.*

When Diane was in this state, I kept a close eye on her, letting her be
alone but always within a short distance of me. She was very content
"taking care" of her little ones. It was painful to watch, but at least she
was content and safe. I would often wonder if she was making
connections with our children, grandchildren, or other children. She
certainly remembered how to care for a child and how to use a mother's
voice to express love and affection.

*I called my banjo teacher today to cancel my banjo lessons until things
get better here. He was very gracious. I'll pick up again as soon as I
can.*

I knew from this point on I wouldn't be able to leave Diane alone at the
house. The banjo lessons were one of those things I was doing for
myself as we learned to do at the caregiver classes. I would have to find
another way to take my mind off things. I could still spend time
practicing and playing banjo at home; I just couldn't bring myself to ask
someone to stay with Diane while I was at lessons. I knew there would
be numerous occasions in the future when I would need to ask someone
to stay with Diane when the demand would be more pressing.

-- Tuesday, October 29, 2013 --

*Diane got to sleep pretty late last night. She woke up around 5:30 AM,
seeing people. I had to sit outside the bathroom door while she
showered. Diane was angry because I didn't sit in the bathroom;
apparently, "they" were in there.*

*Diane couldn't button her blouse this morning--it took a long time.
There are people, bugs, and other unidentified things moving all over
the house. While eating, Diane takes a spoon of cereal then goes into a
room to see what or who is there. She carried the milk carton and
cereal into the living room before I could catch her. She just went into*

45

our bedroom and was mad at "the kids" for getting the good pillows wet. I had to show her the pillows were dry. Now she is scolding someone: Don, our son, and Mona Thompson, a girl who lived in Diane's hometown of Northfield and went to school with us. Now someone is getting into the pie crust by the puzzle on the table. WOW!

Twice this morning Diane has lashed out at me. There is no reason, but it still hurts.

Diane was very mild mannered. In the 52 years we were married, she had never uttered a cross word to me, nor I to her. I knew there were a lot of "miss-connections" being made in her brain. This wasn't the Diane I knew doing these strange things, telling me to shut up, that I was lying, swearing at me, and physically pushing me aside. The words still hurt a lot. I was torn between two powerful and contrasting emotions: first, accepting the condition of dementia, and second, losing the Diane I had known all my life.

Don was up late in the afternoon and stayed until 9:30 PM. Diane was totally non-functional. It was very difficult for Don to see his mother in this state. He is checking in on us daily from now on.

During Don's visit Diane was moving around the house talking in a high-pitched "mother's voice" to a pillow she had wrapped in a blanket, which she said was a baby. She was constantly moving from room to room, talking to children. We just had to let her act out her behaviors.

This was a long night.

It is difficult to say what she was looking for, but when Diane found nothing, she quickly moved to another place to look again. Diane ended up in the bedroom where all the kids' toys were and found the pillow and blanket that became her little baby. She moved about the house talking to the pillow-baby and to her coat rack "friends." Speaking to her had no effect. It was as if her mind was totally focused on the hallucinations.

As Diane continued her strange behavior, Don and I talked about her condition. I explained to Don what I was observing before and after the Risperidone. Because Diane and I are so introverted, we pretty much kept what was going on at our house between the two of us. At that time, I was the only one who really knew the severity of Diane's dementia-induced behavior. It was very difficult for Don.

-- Wednesday, October 30, 2013 --

I cleaned up and put away all the "stuff" Diane brought out from the grandkids' play box last night. She was surprisingly incoherent last evening while Don was here. She saw other people wherever she looked and engaged them in conversation. They never answered; they just "went away."

I'm supposed to have caregiver class today, but I will check in by phone. It is too short notice to get someone to be with Diane at this point.

Today we start Exelon (Rivastigmine) twice per day. This is a level 4 drug according to our insurance company and costs $160 per prescription. We are still keeping Sertraline (anti-depressant) at the previous levels once in the morning.

I had a good cry at 8:00 this morning. I needed that!

"Having a good cry" became a more and more regular event in my life. I think the best way to describe this is by using a pressurized vessel analogy: witnessing the bizarre effects of Diane's dementia, dealing with insurance companies, keeping up with the daily chores, trying to accept that things weren't going to get better for Diane, all built up "pressure in the vessel" that, if not relieved, would explode. The pressure relief, crying, would occur at random times, but I would always try to hold back when Diane was close enough to hear me or see me.

I'm going to remove all the throw rugs today and put the potent meds in a safe place. I need to get a small lockable box.

Diane's depth perception and sense of balance made it difficult for her to change directions when walking. It seemed particularly difficult for her to see things near the floor. One of the suggestions made at the caretaker class was to remove all the smaller rugs on the floor to avoid stumbling over them. I also moved some of the furniture so that there were large open spaces for Diane to move about in.

Diane slept until 10:45 AM today. She was confused about having to wait for a guy before taking a shower and changing her ostomy bag. I helped her, but she didn't want me to be in the bathroom, so I left. Diane did just fine in the bathroom with showering and changing her ostomy bag. She took her first Rivastigmine at approximately 12:15 PM.

-- Thursday, October 31, 2013 --

It's Halloween Day. We are making lasagna for dinner. Greg, Laurie, and Addy will be here also. Addy will be handing out candy after she comes back from trick-or-treating.

Diane woke up at 5:30 AM this morning. She says we are in a camp of some kind, and I've been "shot up" with drugs too many times. She asked me to shut her bedroom door and knock on it three times when I finished in the bathroom. There is still much confusion and hallucinations.

I had a good conversation with Gloria from the Office on Aging. She also teaches our caregiver class. We talked about having Diane come to a coffee session in Barron where about six to eight people with Alzheimer's Disease have structured time from 10 AM to 3 PM with Wisconsin certified Alzheimer's Disease caregivers. I would love to see her try this, but it was very hard to get her to go to our Bible Study with people she has known for years.

Diane and I talked for a long time in the afternoon. I couldn't help breaking down while explaining my role as a caregiver. This was very hard, but we both needed to talk. I don't know how much Diane comprehended, but she seemed very understanding about Alzheimer's Disease and my desire to take good care of her.

48

In rare moments, Diane would seem more "normal" than usual and I cherished these moments. This was one. I remember she asked about her dementia and what I had found in my "constant Internet research," as she put it. I explained what I found out about Alzheimer's disease, as that is what I was researching at the time. I also explained the progression of Parkinson's Disease and how that would affect her ability to move her arms and legs and eventually lead to difficulty swallowing. She asked many questions. I'm sure we talked for over two hours. During this entire time she seemed to understand everything I was saying. I could tell she understood just by the depth of questions she was asking. Just how much she might remember? That was another thing.

This was one of those times when I couldn't hold back crying in Diane's presence.

-- Saturday, November 2, 2013 --

I slept in until 7 AM this morning. We both had a restful night.

When I gave Diane a hug as she was waking up, I asked how she was. "I'm still a little confused," she admitted. It is interesting that she realized that she is confused. So far, no bad side effects from the Rivastigmine.

We went to Rice Lake and bought Diane a new simple watch, as her other two watches didn't run anymore.

Even though time was confusing to her, Diane wanted a watch she could read easily. Her other watches were quite small, and I think they were very difficult for her to see. I was happy to get her something she wanted, as her wants had always been few. It was also good to get her out of the house, even if it was just to go shopping.

Early signs of Capgras Syndrome

-- Sunday, November 3, 2013 --

I need to be at church at 7:30 AM this morning so I got up at 5:50 AM. When I got out of the shower, Diane had the bed made and was dressed, ready for church. Right now she doesn't know what church we go to or where it is.

Oh Lord, Diane asked if I was taking care of her after he died. I asked her who "he" was and she said, "Jim." Then all of a sudden she said, "Oh, you're Jim," realizing I was there.

This little episode slipped by me at the time. Diane was talking to someone, but I didn't know who. She asked this "someone" if they were taking care of her after "Jim" died. It was obvious from her realization that I was Jim. It was me who would possibly die. This was another case of Capgras Syndrome in its early stage. There were definitely two Jims in her mind. As I experienced the effects of dementia in Diane, strange words and actions became the expected. But, at this time, I didn't know there was such a thing as Capgras Syndrome.

Diane and I have talked more in the last few weeks then we ever have. It's just...nothing makes sense. UGH!

-- Monday, November 4, 2013 --

It was good to wake up to a little morning light after setting the clocks back to Standard Time. I did my exercises and spent some research time on Alzheimer's Disease. I find myself doing lots of "research" these days.

Tonight Diane couldn't figure out that I was her husband. This disease stinks!

I knew from my reading that there would possibly be a time when Diane wouldn't recognize me as her husband; however, the first time that occurred it was a shock to my system. We had been together for 55 years, married for 52 years, shared a lifetime of memories, and now Diane didn't recognize me as her husband. Anyone who thinks that isn't a major blow to the psyche is mistaken.

Our wedding picture, June 30, 1963

Laurie and Addy came over and made canvas covers for the windows and pictures so the reflections from these wouldn't confuse Diane. That helped a lot.

Diane would see people, animals, and outdoor scenes in reflections from glass picture frames, doors and windows. It didn't matter what time of the day it was. I read about how reflections often confuse people with dementia, and this was certainly the case with Diane. This disease makes perception difficult, particularly seeing in three dimensions. I envisioned it as being in a virtual world with 3-D goggles. Someone with dementia doesn't need the software and goggles--everything is being played out in the brain in real-time. It is easy to see how Diane could be confused by reflections, stumble over throw rugs, lose her balance getting in and out

51

of a chair, hear other people in a room, or drop something not knowing exactly what she might be bending over to pick up.

Reflections that confused Diane

-- Tuesday, November 5, 2013 --

We didn't go out anywhere today. Diane had a pretty good day. We did have to completely cover the large eagle picture in the living room entry way. As Diane would look at the picture, she would see other people, and they moved. In reality it was her own reflection. Just another manifestation of this disease.

Diane would often call me over to see how the person in the "window" moved. She was particularly sensitive to reflections at night. Even when we covered the painting, Diane would walk up and pull the sheet back to point out to me the things she was seeing. It seemed to help if I would turn a light on and off to show her it was just a reflection.

The MRI was at noon in Rice Lake. It was not a pleasant experience for Diane. She didn't like the noise, but the operator said she did very well.

Diane worked on the puzzle for quite a while today. It's coming but is a very difficult puzzle.

Don checked in around 8:00 PM. I really appreciate his calls.

We went to bed a little after 9 PM. Diane didn't want to be alone with "all these people around."

It was always a relief to talk to someone about the day, so Don's nightly calls were important. But the best part was to engage in normal conversation. I didn't have to try to explain reflections, answer repetitive questions, try to put myself in Diane's head to help her understand something, or not tell the truth about something to satisfy a delusion. Don's "checking in conversations" were definitely a form of therapy.

-- Wednesday, November 6, 2013 --

There is a lot of confusion again this morning about this "guy" who is simultaneous "owner" of our house. This is a constant theme all day and night.

The issues with two houses were compounded by a simultaneous "owner" of these houses who had identical legal papers to ours and was trying to take away our ownership of the house by changing the documents to show he was the real owner. I spent countless hours answering questions about the authenticity and accuracy of the documents. I went through my usual routine of getting our satisfaction of deed out of the fireproof safe to show her everything was indeed in order. Seeing the actual document would satisfy her for a couple of hours, but then the questions would start over again.

Now there were two houses, more than one of me, and a mystery "guy" who was trying to gain ownership of our house. I was having difficulty keeping everything straight in my mind! It is astounding how the brain works through hallucinations, delusions, paranoia, misconceptions, misperceptions, and faulty logic to present a pseudo world to one with dementia, a world that is all too real to them.

I went to my caregivers class at 1:30 PM today. Louise, a good friend for years, came to be with Diane while I was at class. This class is very helpful, and I'm learning a lot about resources available locally as well as nationally.

The resources suggested by the caregivers class were excellent. These, in addition to the Internet sites for Alzheimer's and Parkinson's Disease, helped me learn what I needed to know about symptoms and prognoses, as well as how others dealt with loved ones who were experiencing the diseases. One thing was certain, I had a lot of reading and research to do.

Diane is totally obsessed with funeral arrangements for someone tonight. Our house had been turned into a mortuary. I never found out who died.

For most of a day Diane would be worried about some "guy" owning our house. A few hours later our house was a mortuary, and we had to make arrangements for a funeral. The "to do" list was long. Were the flowers ordered? Did someone call the pastor? Who's going to tell the family about the funeral? While she had no idea who the funeral was for, it was clear we were both experiencing a death of sorts within these four walls. But our house, like a mortuary, had a viewing area, a place for family and guests to meet, and a chapel. I don't think I was a good undertaker for Diane's funeral home.

-- Friday, November 8, 2013 --

Diane has so much trouble with the concept of our house being sold, taken, or moved. Again, the entire section of town has been "moved from a hill down to this place." There is this "person," who is "Jim Adams," who looks just like me but is the one trying to scam us out of our house. Diane returns to this idea over and over.

The instantaneous moving of our house had expanded to the entire neighborhood. According to Diane, "our house," which was on a hill, along with the entire neighborhood, was moved to where we were. It all happened in the blink of an eye. Along with the neighborhood relocation, there was this other person named "Jim Adams." He looked just like me and acted like me, but he was trying to scam us out of our house. I would spend hours answering questions as she tested me on my knowledge of who was in charge, who signed the papers, how much it cost, how much money was transferred from our account, only to once again face Diane's disbelief. I was indeed the scam artist trying to take our house away. I would constantly try to change the subject or distract her by leaving the room and returning a short time later. It never worked. While the logic and memory paths in Diane's brain were somehow misdirected, they were indeed persistent.

-- Sunday, November 10, 2013 --

Diane and I watched the church service on the computer; it's good to be able to do this.

We went outside and raked the leaves under the trees. It was the first nice day we have had in sometime.

Raking leaves is something Diane always enjoyed doing. She liked getting outside and always enjoyed looking at a freshly raked lawn. It was an excellent activity for her because there wasn't a multiple step process involved. We would rake for a little while and then sit on the front steps in the warm sunlight and rest. Diane had a few problems coordinating the use of two rakes to pick up leaves and put them into the leaf bag. Little did I realize this would be the last time we would rake leaves together.

-- Monday, November 11, 2013 --

Diane was quite confused while we were working on the puzzle. She was always wondering where Greg was. She again asked about whether her dad was going to pick someone up. Diane's deceased parents often come up in her thinking now.

When I came to bed tonight the door was shut, and Diane was concerned about others in the house. She had also gone to bed early, in her normal clothes. When I asked her if she wanted to get her pajamas on, she said, "OK," and changed into them.

Diane's dad Norman and mother Thea

-- Tuesday, November 12, 2013 --

Diane woke up quite confused today. Again, other people were in the house: two little girls this time.

Diane has also returned to seeing me as the guy who looks like me but wants to take our house away.

We worked on the puzzle for a long time today. Diane was continually wondering where her sister Cleo was.

Diane helped me fix dinner tonight. She fixed frozen peas and carrots, which were done 45 minutes before the chicken and potatoes. Diane has no sense of time. I love having her with me in the kitchen. It's good for both of us.

It was great to have Diane actively working her hands and mind in the kitchen. She would often ask me why the clock seemed to "jump all over the place." I did have to be very careful about Diane using sharp knives, as her ability to make small movements was impaired by the Parkinson's (if this is Parkinson's). Her hand motions were quite slow but deliberate. It certainly wasn't the Diane I was used to seeing in the kitchen. She used to plan an entire meal, prepare fresh fruit and vegetables, use her hands to lay down a perfect lasagna layer, time the preparation of dishes so that everything was done at the proper time, slice, pour, place silverware in the proper order on the table, and present a delicious meal that couldn't be beat by any TV chef. Diane's better-than-bakery chocolate chip cookies and ice cream topped off many exquisite meals. Now, she could barely prepare a frozen dinner.

-- Wednesday, November 13, 2013 --

I read the rest of chapter 4 in my caregivers handbook and went to class at 1:30 PM, while Chris and her kids stayed with Diane. The class was excellent, as usual, but it ran a little long.

This particular class focused on redirecting dementia patients to get their thoughts on another track. There was a lot of great sharing from the participants, but I slowly lost my concentration. I was thinking about how Chris was doing with Diane and the little ones. I don't know why I was so worried about the time. Time meant nothing to Diane.

After dinner, as Chris and I were sitting in the living room, we heard a "thump" in the kitchen. We all rushed in to find Diane on the floor between the stove and refrigerator. She had another dizzy spell and hit her elbow and side on the counter as she fell. She was not pale or clammy like fainting.

The thud and thump of someone falling on a floor is very distinct. Diane was sitting on the floor with her back leaning against the lower cupboards. At first she seemed kind of lost, but by the time I got to her she was trying to get up off the floor. Chris and I helped her up. I used techniques I had read about on the Internet to help her get back on her feet, being careful to use my legs and arms to lift so I wouldn't hurt my back (that "endless research" was coming in handy).

Knowing what we were dealing with

-- Friday, November 15, 2013 --

I did my usual exercises about 6:45 AM. I also read some humor in the **Over 60 Joke Book.** *The old George Burns jokes are still pretty funny.*

We were talking about humor in the caregiver class and how important it is to laugh during the difficult times while caring for someone with dementia. One of our tasks was to read something humorous during the week.

Diane woke up about 8:15 this morning. She has been concerned for Chris and the babies this morning.

We went to see the doctor in Rice Lake. We finally know what we are dealing with: <u>not</u> Alzheimer's but Lewy Body Dementia with Parkinson's Disease. The MRI showed a considerable shrinkage of brain matter and significant reduction in the lining area where Parkinson's Disease is visible. The latest symptoms also match very well the Lewy Bodies Disease symptoms. The brain MRI also showed that Diane had a small stroke at some earlier time. It was not possible to know how long ago this might have been.

It was striking to see the large darkened areas indicating shrinkage. The doctor informed us that Lewy Body Dementia often moves faster than Alzheimer's and when coupled with Parkinson's will lead to things like difficulty swallowing, joint muscle degradation, poor balance, etc. Diane is still in excellent spirits.

I remember questioning the match between what I was reading regarding Alzheimer's Disease and the symptoms Diane was exhibiting. Most sources pointed out that each person is different, and individual symptoms are likely to vary considerably. I was very relieved to know precisely what we were dealing with. Being an engineer I need to know all the details about what I observe. That feeling was intensified as it pertained to what was happening to my wife. My research had a new direction.

I had been looking at pictures of Alzheimer's Disease MRI's. When I first saw Diane's MRI pictures I knew there were problems. It brought me back to the photos I saw on the doctor's desk after Diane had the colonoscopy, just before being diagnosed with colon cancer. I knew things were not right. I could see white clumps of matter in the intestine. I remember my heart sinking, feeling that deep sense of "this doesn't look good." The same feeling came to me as I looked at Diane's brain MRI. There were numerous dark areas where there should have been shades of gray. My first thoughts were focused on the extent of damage the dementia had already done to the brain.

I had never heard of Lewy Body Dementia, so my Internet research began immediately after getting home. The Lewy Body Dementia Association, Inc., web site (https://www.lbda.org) was of great help. I highly recommend it as a major resource for understanding the disease.

-- Saturday, November 16, 2013 --

Diane's side, where she fell against the refrigerator on Wednesday, was hurting today when she stood up or sat down. She thinks she laid on that side during the night.

"Sundowning" made its usual appearance this evening. Diane is still confused about our house location, ownership, and how everything got "moved" here from "downtown."

Sundowning, as I learned from our caregiver class, comes from the time of day when dementia seems to heighten. This was very true with Diane. Each day, late into the afternoon and during the evening, she would show increased symptoms of dementia. For example, around 5 PM Diane would start to see people in the reflections of glassed surfaces, start wandering around the house looking for something or somebody, or start questioning me about the location of our house. "Sundowning" became a regular occurrence and signaled the start of the toughest part of the day.

Cleo called tonight. She and Diane talked for a while. I explained the Lewy body dementia and Parkinson's to her the best I could.

Diane's sister Cleo

I told Cleo over a million people have this disease, so it is quite common but often misdiagnosed as Alzheimer's disease. It is difficult to explain what Lewy bodies are: abnormal protein deposits that interfere with normal brain functions. These protein deposits interfere with the synapses and neurons where brain communication occurs. It's how the brain makes connections with its various functions like visual, audio, logic, bodily movement, etc. Lewy bodies form groups in the neurons and interfere with the workings of the neurons and eventually causes them to die. I told Cleo that this will cause changes in information processing, language, perception, emotion, behavior, ability to create new memory, bodily movement, sleeping and even recognizing smells.

I also explained that the disease lasts anywhere from five to seven years on average but can vary between two and 20 years. We had no idea where Diane was in this time spectrum but knew she had symptoms for possibly more than a year. I further explained that the Parkinson's Disease was causing Diane to lose her balance and fall periodically. So, the disruption and ultimate destruction of brain communication in conjunction with the Parkinson's Disease was not a good prognosis. Eventually, I told Cleo, Diane would no longer be able to swallow.

Cleo said she would pass the word to Diane's other brothers and sisters.

-- Monday, November 18, 2013 --

Today we take Diane up to a support group meeting in Barron. We'll see how it goes. I'll stay with her as long as she wants me to.

We spent the morning at the support group in Barron (9 AM to 12:30 PM). We had lunch there before we left. It's hard to get a read on how Diane felt. She said she had mixed feelings. She liked the Thanksgiving activity, the pastor, and the singing parts, but she didn't have much to converse about with the other guests. That's understandable. I think she might want to go back on a Wednesday or Friday when there are fewer people attending. She did smile, laugh, and help with putting things away after lunch. We'll have to talk some more later to see if she wants to go back.

Diane stayed very close to me during the support group. The only time she left me was when she helped pick up dishes after the lunch. This was what she always did whenever we ate lunch at someone else's house: she helped get the dishes ready for washing. I too had a tough time finding something to talk about with those at the table. I could tell that she wasn't very enthused with the visit. I didn't press the thought of going back until several days later.

Learning about grief

I didn't exercise this morning. I started a beef dish in the slow cooker just in case Chris and the little ones want to have dinner here. They will stay with Diane when I'm in my caregiver class.

We talked about emotions in class today. My emotional observation was grieving, knowing I am slowly losing the person I love so much.

I never thought about grieving before we read and talked about it in class. At this point I was just trying to get up to speed on Lewy Bodies and Parkinson's Disease. But I was definitely experiencing grief. I could see Diane slipping away from reality. It was always in the back of my mind that Diane wasn't going to be with me very long. I didn't know how long, only that she wouldn't be with me. That caused me much grief. I wasn't to the point of experiencing a lot of weeping or depression. Things were happening very rapidly, and I had all I could do to keep up with being a caregiver.

I got home a little before 4 PM. Chris said Diane was really good today. There wasn't as much confusion as in the last few times. I'm thankful for days like this.

I would pray constantly for Diane to have days with less confusion. I think having Chris and the little grandchildren around all afternoon really helped Diane. It is common for people with dementia to do much better when they are around others. In caregiver terms it is known as "showtime," when people with dementia want to do their best to show others they don't have problems. Witnessing Diane's "showtime" caused me to question my skills as a caregiver. I was with her continuously but observed no "showtime" when things seemed better for her. Why couldn't I do something to cause this heightened alertness on a daily basis? I came to realize that Diane and I lived with the dementia 24/7 and there was no need for a "showtime." But, when others were around, that was a different story indeed. Diane simply wanted to show others she was OK, a natural thing for her to do.

-- Thursday, November 21, 2013 --

Diane and I went to Rice Lake to pick up a large calendar for 2013, among other things.

Diane was having a real problem reading the wall calendar in the kitchen. I asked her if she would like a large calendar that we could put on the side of the refrigerator that had bigger boxes for appointments. She thought that would be a good idea. We found a desk top calendar and hung it up on the side of the refrigerator. It helped. We could write much larger for Diane to see. She could also count the days a lot easier.

-- Friday, November 22, 2013 --

Diane took a very long nap this morning. She was really tired. We had a very "do nothing day." We need these once in awhile.

One of the symptoms of Lewy Body Dementia is sleeping more in the daytime. Diane had always taken naps when she could. But she was sleeping much more during the day. Sometimes she would sleep for a couple of hours. When this happened, I was able to read, do Internet research, or go downstairs to work on my model airplane. It gave me a break. I'm sure it's the same kind of feeling Diane had when, as a stay-at-home mom, she could take a much needed parenting break while the children were napping.

-- Saturday, November 23, 2013 --

Today is lefse making day at Don and Heidi's.

Making lefse, a Scandinavian flatbread made of potatoes, flour, cream, and butter, is a laborious process. Lefse making days have been a tradition in our family for many years. Everyone has a part in the lefse baking and, of course, everyone gets to have fresh lefse as a treat. Most of us eat it with lots of butter and sugar rolled up inside. Others eat it with butter only or with Lutefisk rolled up inside.

This was a familiar setting for Diane as she had made lefse with her sisters for years. She always did the baking of the lefse on the grill. She would watch the lefse and when little brown spots appeared on the bottom and air pockets appeared on top she would slide the lefse stick under it and gently turn it over to bake on the other side.

This year was quite different. It took longer for Diane to roll the lefse from the lefse stick onto the grill. She had to be reminded where to put the finished rounds. Just moving the few steps from the grill to the where the finished lefse was placed was a challenge. Her movement was very slow and deliberate throughout the day. There was always lighthearted conversation and it was good to see Diane smile and laugh with all of us. We all did our best to make this event as normal as possible, not letting Lewy Body Dementia interfere with this family tradition. This day was one of those treasured moments of joy--a time of triumph over dementia.

-- Sunday, November 24, 2013 --

I watched the church service on the Internet. Diane slept in but thought it was the day we go to Brenda's for Thanksgiving--that's next Saturday, the 30th.

I practiced banjo while Diane was watching a movie. When I finished I walked into the living room. Diane said, "Where did you come from?"

I said, "I've been practicing the banjo and just walked in here."

She said, "You didn't. How did you get in here?"

I explained and turned the dining room lights on, but that didn't seem to help. She went to look out the front door window. She asked me where I had been. I said I was practicing banjo. She said, "That was a long time ago." Diane is quite mixed up this evening.

This is a mean disease! Diane's sense of time and place is getting worse by the week.

-- Thursday, November 28, 2013 --

Thanksgiving day. There is so much to be thankful for: Diane, our children, grandchildren, a warm place to sleep, good and plentiful food and much more.

-- Saturday, November 30, 2013 --

We arrived in Whitehall, WI, about noon for the Nelson Thanksgiving dinner. It was good to see everyone again. I talked at length with Mel and his daughter Calla. Diane spent some time with her sister Norma. Of course, we spent time talking with Chris as she cared for little Reuben.

During this gathering Diane didn't move about much but sat talking with her sisters and brothers most of the time. It gets quite noisy when everyone is talking, so it was hard for Diane to hear some of the conversation. She listened, smiled and even laughed often. As I watched her, she was interacting well. To see her one would think there was nothing wrong. It was a perfect example of "showtime." It was wonderful to see Diane doing so well, one of those answers to prayer.

Diane fell again tonight. I was in the kitchen putting dishes into the washer when I heard a loud thump. I rushed into the living room and found Diane had fallen between her chair and the wall. She knocked down the reading lamp and hit her right side again. I helped her up, and she sat down on the couch. She said she felt like she was "floating." I think it also has to do with sudden rotational movements when she gets up from a chair.

When someone you love so much falls like this, it's a "gut-wrenching" experience. I felt so bad I wasn't there to catch her before she landed on the floor. It happened so fast and so unexpectedly that it was impossible to catch her in the act. Tears came to my eyes every time she fell. I just hugged her and held her until she was ready to get up. Each time she got up after one of these incidents she told me, "It feels like I'm floating."

65

It turns out that her falling was due to a lowering of blood pressure when she suddenly got up from a chair after sitting for an extended time. I think the lack of balance due to the Parkinson's also contributed.

Diane has fallen three times since September 25th, 2013. It's difficult to know if the dizzy spells are a result of the drugs she is taking or from the Parkinson's Disease.

-- Sunday, December 1, 2013 --

I practiced the banjo while Diane watched a movie. After the movie she re-arranged her new purse again. This is a regular activity. I've purchased three purses in the past few months.

One of Diane's continuous activities was to transfer contents from one purse to another. She just couldn't find the right purse for all her things. We would visit the purse section of a department store each time we were there. Once in awhile she would feel that one of the purses she saw would do the trick, and we would buy it. When we got home she would sit on the couch and transfer all the belongings from her "old purse" to the new one. A few days later she would sit on the couch and transfer the items from the new purse to one of her older purses. I think she had five or six purses that she used continuously in this manner. I didn't mind purchasing new purses; it was such a minor thing she loved. Actually, I would have done anything for her.

-- Monday, December 2, 2013 --

I left Diane alone while I went to take the recyclables downtown, mail the bills, get gas for the snow thrower, and pay the Internet bill. Diane was sitting at the table when I got back, exactly where I left her.

I would not leave Diane alone for long periods of time. At this stage of her dementia, I would leave her for periods of less than half an hour. Even then, it was uncomfortable, and I would get the errands done as quickly as possible. I do remember being quite surprised to see that Diane was sitting there exactly where I left her.

Diane fell again today. I was downstairs on the computer when I heard a large thump. I ran upstairs to find Diane on the floor between two chairs. I let her rest on the floor a while and asked if she could try to get up on her own. She crawled to the blue rocker/recliner, pulled herself up and sat in the chair. She had been napping and was getting up to see who was at the back door. Diane heard me do some pounding downstairs and thought it was someone knocking at the back door.

Five or six hammer strikes, then nothing while I reached for another nail, then five or six more strikes. I had no clue that this would affect Diane in any way. But it did, and I became very sensitive to pounding or doing anything in the shop that might cause Diane to think there was someone at the door.

Diane doesn't seem to pass out during her falls. She describes it like flying or floating. I'm thinking of purchasing a baby monitor and placing it in the living room so I can monitor sounds while I'm downstairs.

I did some research on baby monitors but decided it wouldn't work because I might not hear the sound while working with noisy tools in the shop.

-- Thursday, December 5, 2014 --

I decorated the Christmas tree after we got home from Rice Lake. It looks nice with the new lights--actually better than any we saw in the stores.

This was the first year Diane didn't help decorate the tree. She was always there helping me put on lights and place decorations. This time I put the tree up by myself. Diane seemed to have little interest in putting up the tree; in fact, she had little interest in the Christmas season. I remember feeling a sense of loss. Diane and I used to work together like a team getting the house decorated. It was a stark realization of what Lewy Body Dementia does to the brain.

Diane had a really difficult time tonight. She was very confused. She was extremely concerned that Bruce, the son of our friends from Colorado, was going to ask her to marry him. She didn't know what to do. I couldn't get her off the subject. Later she did know that Jim Adams was her husband, but I was not him. Lewy Body Dementia sucks!

The proper brain connections couldn't be made because the Lewy Bodies protein clumps prevented information from moving to the proper places. If the information can't move in the normal path, it seems to take another. This new path involved a marriage proposal. This confused Diane, and she didn't know what to do. She knew Bruce asking her to marry him was wrong but couldn't come up with a solution in her mind. I remember telling her I would try to call Bruce to tell him she didn't want to marry him.

-- Friday, December 6, 2013 --

It's very cold this morning: 0 degrees. Diane wanted to know where everyone was this morning. She thought the "kids" were here. Sometimes the "kids" are our children and other times they are boy scouts or school kids. Because of the "kids" or other people she is reluctant to take a shower or to wear only pajamas to bed.

-- Saturday, December 7, 2013 --

I'll finish decorating for Christmas today and hopefully spend some time on the Taylorcraft.

I put up Diane's collection of Santas this morning. That always completes the holiday look around the house.

Diane read the paper a while tonight. She still believes we are living in a shared apartment or housing development of some kind. I answered questions for at least an hour about the appliances and who repairs them, the permission required to make changes, whether we can afford the rent, meeting with change committees, etc. Ugh!

It is almost impossible to change subjects, as we come right back to the same issues.

We lived in apartments decades ago while I was in engineering school in California, while I worked for NASA in Texas, and while I worked as a civilian for the Air Force in Ohio. But, according to Diane's mind, we were living in some kind of apartment complex or housing development. She would question me about our ability to afford such a nice apartment. I would have to go over our paycheck with her and make sure I always had plenty left for savings. I was, according to Diane's mind, a member of the "change committee" at the apartment complex and telling her about the meetings we had and what I had learned about new rules.

These "conversations" were often difficult to manage. It was like writing a real-time script for a play. Even though she could no longer work with numbers, I would have to print a hard copy of our budget spreadsheet so Diane could see that we could afford to live where she thought we were living. We never argued about the budget. Diane seemed to be okay as long as I could justify the spending. It was almost impossible to distract or change subjects when she was in this frame of mind. I remember how mentally tiring it was.

-- Monday, December 9, 2013 --

Diane's hallucinations were pretty pronounced tonight. I put away the stuffed Christmas animals and a Christmas pillow that were giving her problems. She didn't want to go to bed, so we sat up until 10:30 PM. The conversation involved the two of us being together, not married, and what we should tell our children.

In addition to glass reflections, Diane would often see pillows or other things that sometimes get moved about in the house as people or animals. In keeping with our family holiday tradition, I placed her collection of stuffed Christmas animals in our living room area. At first they didn't seem to bother her. But as sundowning time approached, these stuffed animals became people. Diane didn't like them. I immediately removed them.

It became obvious that Diane was seeing me as another person, not her husband, which was confirmed when she began to worry about our living together. She was very sensitive about our not being married. How we would explain our relationship to people? How should we tell the kids? She was worried that they might abandon us if they found out we were living together and weren't married. Even the idea, "It's not Diane, it's the disease," couldn't alleviate the hurt of not being recognized as her husband.

-- Thursday, December 12, 2013 --

I spent about half an hour reading from a book on dementia. It is rather long but covers much of what I'm seeing and what I'm expecting to see in the future. Big help!

Diane woke up and was expecting to go to a "Nelson" funeral. There was a funeral announcement over the radio this morning for a Nelson, and she must have assumed it was for a relative. It turns out she was thinking the funeral was for Mary Bergerson who passed away many years ago.

Tonight was really tough. The "other" Jim Adams was doing all kinds of things. He was coming to pick Diane up, and she doesn't want him around. He is trying to take our house away. He has memorized our life events so when she talks to him he knows everything about her and the family. Diane wanted to get out of the house by just "walking home"; however, she didn't know where home was.

As time progressed the manifestation of her disease took an unexpected and unwelcome turn: the "other" Jim Adams became more aggressive in terms of bad behavior. Diane disliked him very much and was sometimes afraid of him. According to Diane, this Jim Adams wanted to take her and our house away. This Jim Adams was a spy. Often she would get me, "a caretaker," mixed up with the "other" Jim Adams and speak to me as if I were indeed the "other" Jim Adams. Diane would accuse me of playing back audio tapes, watching family movies, reading family letters, and memorizing family facts to make her believe I was *her* Jim Adams. She would become very terse, treating me as if I were a complete stranger. She wanted no part of me. Then, in the blink of an eye, I would become her caretaker again with concerns over our living together and not being married.

A very bad month

-- Friday, December 13, 2013 --

Diane came into the kitchen as I was doing dishes. Today she was concerned about somebody stealing the figurines from the nativity scene. She wanted them packed up and put back in the box. I did that while she was showering. I may have to remove the Christmas tree also, as it confuses her in the evenings. We'll see.

Diane and I had a VERY rough day. She had hallucinations of boy scouts running all over the house and stealing things. She became very disturbed when I tried to help her understand there were no Boy Scouts and our house wasn't a scout camp.

The Christmas tree bothered Diane, so I took it down. She helped me for a while but then began to gather up the pictures of the grandchildren and some small figurines so she could "take them home."

Then the "other Jim Adams" came into the picture again. She is afraid of this person. It's difficult to know if she can tell which Jim Adams is with her at a given time. The "bad" Jim Adams is divorced from her. The "good" Jim Adams is living with her. She feels guilty about that and is often worried about how we are going to tell the kids we are living together. Today she is asking about our wedding date and if we were going to send invitations soon. She is not recognizing that I am her husband. That hurts.

I think taking down the Christmas tree and her gathering up things in the house was very stressful for me. I cried all the time I vacuumed, cleaning up from the removal of the tree. I cried hard!

When I finished in our bedroom Diane came into the hallway. Right away she wondered what was wrong. I just hugged her tightly and cursed Lewy Body Dementia telling her I was upset about losing her to this "damned disease." She did all she could to comfort me.

72

***This was a VERY emotional day. I'm taking it as preparation for
things to come.***

I put the Christmas tree up on December 5, 2013. After it was up Diane
would move toward it and examine the many tree decorations. She
would put her hands on a decoration, feeling it and looking at it as if she
had never seen it before. Then she would move to another decoration
and do the same. The tree itself didn't seem to bother her the first few
days, but as she moved around the house she would look at the tree and
see a person. When I put the lights on to show her that it was only the
Christmas tree, she would move away from it. Clearly the lights
bothered her and caused confusion. I imagined it to be similar to the
reflections in glass that bothered her so much. The more I thought about
it the more I realized the tree had to be taken down and put away.

It was an emotional thing to be taking the tree down weeks before
celebrating Christmas. We've had a Christmas tree in the house since
both of us were babies. To me this seemed a huge loss.

The next to go was our small nativity scene we had set out for many
years during the weeks of Advent. Diane was extremely concerned that
someone was going to steal the figurines. She persisted in her demands
that I remove them from the room and put them back in the closet. I
agreed.

Our house has framed family photos on lamp tables, shelves, and on the
walls. We also have figurines that we were given as gifts over the years.
All these items were valuable to Diane, and in her fear of someone
taking them, she spent the day gathering each item and putting the
collection in a clothes basket in the bedroom. She even removed some of
the wall decorations and put them into the basket. Diane was very
deliberate and careful, carrying only two items at a time. She didn't want
the Scouts in the house to get their hands on these things.

I knew the Lewy Body Dementia was causing my heightened emotions.
This really upset me. I was losing--had, in fact, lost--my life partner to
Lewy Body Dementia. This Friday the 13th was for me, a truly unlucky
day. That was the day I accepted the fact that I had lost the Diane I
loved so very much. It was like receiving a phone call telling me that

Diane had been killed in an accident. I couldn't hold back the tears as I was putting the tree and boxes back in the basement.

After vacuuming the floors I was in the hallway winding the cord up. Diane surprised me and could see instantly that I was crying. She hugged me tightly and tried her best to console me. I don't remember her saying anything; just hugging me and holding me was enough. We held each other for a long time, long enough for my crying to subside.

-- Saturday, December 14, 2013 --

I read for a while this morning. Diane started to get ready about 8 AM. I'm still emotionally drained from yesterday, but I'll be fine.

I spent some time downstairs in the shop working on the Taylorcraft. I REALLY needed that time to get my mind off Lewy Body Dementia for a while.

Around dinner the "apartment vs. home" issues surfaced again, along with two other "Jim Adams" in Diane's mind. Now there are two besides me, very interesting indeed. She wanted to pack her stuff and "go home" tonight. That would be to Northfield to stay with her mom. Diane did finally realize that her mom Thea passed away many years ago. These evenings are very hard on both of us.

It was very difficult to know which Jim Diane was conversing with at any given time. This made it almost impossible to try to get inside her thoughts and carry on a conversation.

Diane's childhood home

-- Friday, December 20, 2013 --

I did my normal exercises and read for a while. We were supposed to go to Daybreak, a senior daycare group, this morning, but yesterday when I mentioned that we were going Diane was not very excited. As I talked more about it with her, I could easily sense she did not want to go. I didn't want to force her in any way, so I called the Barron County Office on Aging and let them know we wouldn't be coming. It seemed to be a relief to Diane. We'll try again in the spring.

I had mentioned the Daybreak group to Diane several times since our earlier visit. She would always change the subject. If I directly asked her if she would like to go again she would usually reply, "I suppose so." I knew how difficult it was for her to relate to others, particularly strangers, and how self-conscious she was about her dementia. I just couldn't take her even if she was doing it to please me. Diane's "I suppose so" means "I'd rather not."

Last night, or rather early this morning, Diane was getting out of bed. I asked her where she was going and she replied, "I don't know." This is the first time she has done this.

This evening was a perfect example of paranoia with Lewy Body. Diane did not recognize me as her husband, which is often the case. Her "thinking" is that I have memorized all the facts about our kids and family in order to steal her money. She was afraid I was going to shoot her. Diane wanted to see our house deed. When I brought the small safe into the room she got very mad and wondered where I had gotten that! She accused me of stealing it.

Paranoia was very common. As we were conversing, Diane would suddenly turn the subject to my (meaning one of the "other Jim's") plans to steal her money from her. She would literally interrogate me, asking how I was able to get information that both of us had known for years. She thought I had recorded everything about our family and memorized it so she would be fooled into giving up her money and the house.

In this particular instance Diane wanted me to prove to her that our house deed was in good order and that there were no liens on the property. Our small fireproof safe was in our bedroom closet, and I brought it out to show her the deed. It is very unusual for Diane to show anger, but she was very angry that I had brought the safe out. She was certain I had stolen it.

More than once she said, "I suppose you are going to kill me." This was always devastating. But to Diane the possibility of my killing her was real; after all, I was not her husband but some imposter trying to steal her money and her house. I would always tell her I would never hurt her in any way and that I loved her very much. Sometimes it would help, other times she would simply say, "Go ahead and kill me."

Diane wanted to go home to her mom and dad. She was asking how she would get there; she was going to walk since she couldn't drive. I finally got her to calm down by talking about how difficult it would be to be outdoors in such cold weather.

I remember being surprised that Diane remembered she couldn't drive. We had taken the car keys away from her shortly after observing symptoms of dementia. She had no problems with the idea that she couldn't drive. But now not driving meant she couldn't get home to her mom and dad on such a cold night. Most of the time when she would want to "go home," I would only have to open the outside door, and the cold air hitting her face would convince her to stay in the house for the night.

When she was wondering how I knew everything about the family, I brought out the "LOVE" book that Chris had made for our 50th wedding anniversary. She looked through the first few pages and asked in a very terse way how I had gotten hold of this information. She thought I had all this information "on tape," that I had memorized everything and made the pictures in the book. LEWY is really messing things up for her. She simply could not accept that I was the father of our children. When I asked her to talk to our children on Christmas day, she said I had programmed them to say what I wanted them to say.

Like the safe that contained the house deed, Diane was very angry that I had somehow gotten my hands on this anniversary book. She also accused me of *making* the pictures, which is understandable since I used to develop and print all our family films and photos. She seemed to recognize the people in the photographs, including her husband, but couldn't relate the images she saw in the book with the person sitting with her in the room at the time. She told me I was not the father of her children.

This was the first time she had implied the kids were also against her. I knew it wasn't Diane saying this, it was Lewy Body Dementia. At the same time, it was very hurtful. I felt a deep sense of loss, the loss of Diane's thinking ability, the loss of her trust in the children, and the loss of her closeness to me. When things like this happen it is like someone reaching inside you and removing part of your being.

-- Tuesday, December 24, 2013 --

After a mentally draining night it's good to feel refreshed and ready for another day dealing with LEWY.

There was an interesting thing this morning: Diane said it was a "George Nelson" who did all the things I wrote about yesterday. She didn't know a George Nelson nor did I. But it is George Nelson, who is now appearing and disappearing, doing bad things.

I've got to find out the difference between hallucinations and delirium. All these brain associated symptoms are very much alike and occur in many brain diseases.

I always tried very hard to "get inside" Diane's head to determine who she thought she was talking with at a given time. I thought last night she was "seeing" and speaking to one of the other Jims. But now there is another person named George Nelson who is the imposter.

Diane and I watched the Christmas eve services from our church on the computer. The church was full. I missed going to a Christmas eve service. This is the first I can ever remember.

-- Wednesday, December 25, 2013 --

We left from Christmas at Don and Heidi's about 4:30 PM. From the time we got on the road until we hit Highway 53, I was bombarded with questions and accusations about who I was and why I was "chosen" to interfere with "everything." It got so bad we both decided to not say anything until we got home.

We had a tearful discussion after we got home (my tears). Discussions mean nothing to LEWY. Diane seems to have little or no sad emotions, but she does smile sometimes.

Diane seemed to interact well with everyone during our Christmas Day, although there was some normal confusion. But as soon as we got into the car Diane began to shoot out questions. I would answer by saying things like, "The kids asked me to do this," or "I wasn't chosen, I was always here." But nothing would satisfy her. Eventually, I couldn't concentrate on driving and answering the barrage of questions. I said, "I think we should just be quiet until we get home." When she would ask another question, I would say, "Not until we get home." Finally, she stopped.

When we got home, I tearfully explained my feelings and what Lewy Body Dementia was doing to our lives. Diane didn't say anything while I was trying to talk and cry at the same time. She didn't show any emotions, just seemed to stare into space. I was "dumping" my frustrations with Lewy Body Dementia while at the same time grieving for the loss of the person I loved.

-- Thursday, December 26, 2013 --

Diane picked up where she left off last night. No recognition of me as her husband and still wanting to "go home." She rolls her eyes when she asks where we are staying next, and I tell her, "Right here in our house." The things I've read about the disease are very accurate: it doesn't do any good to argue with someone with dementia. It's impossible to communicate with a brain that has lost its ability to use logical reasoning.

I spent most of the day gathering materials on our financial accounts, insurance policies, medical powers of attorney, etc. I want to have these ready when Don, Greg, and Chris come tomorrow to discuss what should be done if something should happen to me. How will we care for Diane?

Having the children here with Diane and me to discuss "what if" situations in case of sudden health changes was something we needed to do, particularly with Diane's declining situation. Diane could give us an idea of what kind of care she preferred when things progressed to that point or if something happened to me. Diane seemed very responsive to my questions regarding her wishes if something should happen to me.

She wanted to be in a smaller house, to be near her brothers and sisters, to have household tasks such as snow removal, lawn work, etc. taken care of. She wanted to make sure Don understood our insurance policies and all the children knew our financial state.

-- Friday, December 27, 2013 --

I still get teary-eyed when I think of what's happened to Diane and all of us in the last four months. I'm trying not to look ahead but take one day at a time. That's hard for me to do.

We had a great session with Don, Greg, and Chris.

Our meeting went very well. Diane sat at the table with us during the entire session. She answered questions from each of us, and I think she understood what we were doing. She kept emphasizing that she wanted to be near her children and brothers and sisters if she had to move. She thought Eau Claire or Chippewa would be a good place to live. I went over the spread sheet that showed all our budgeting, savings, investments, and insurance. We discussed the power of attorney and living will documents. We also went over the pre-arranged funeral wishes and documents.

The kids were great, even though it might have been uncomfortable discussing some of the items. Having this meeting gave me a great sense of relief knowing that each of them knew of our end of life wishes, healthcare wishes, and financial condition.

I gave each of them a copy of our financial documents and agreed to download Wisconsin legal forms for my power of attorney, medical care wishes, disposition of body, etc., take them to our lawyer to modify and get copies to each of them. I also told Don I would make a "for Don" folder on my computer downstairs that would contain all the documents we talked about today. I also would have a list of all my computer accounts and their passwords.

-- Monday, December 30, 2013 --

While I was practicing banjo tonight Diane stood by the door and said she was concerned because she had forgotten to make funeral arrangements. When I asked who the funeral was for she said, "For my husband." I told her I hadn't seen any death announcement in the paper, and that seemed to satisfy her.

I remember asking Diane when her husband died. She said she didn't know. It is such a weird thing to have your own wife talking to you about your own nonexistent death. Yet, Diane was talking to me (whichever "me" she thought I was) as if her husband's death were a fact.

-- Tuesday, December 31, 2013 --

Diane is still concerned about a funeral but doesn't know who it is for. She said someone was playing banjo last night just like her dad (her dad never played banjo as far as I know). She didn't know who, just some guy. She said the guy was really good and played the same music as her dad. How about that--I'm pretty good!

During late morning/early afternoon the "bad Jim Adams" was on Diane's mind. She was very negative toward anything he, meaning me, said. Finally around two o'clock I went outside to get the mail and shovel snow from the driveway. As I was putting on my boots and coat, she accused me of using Jim's coat and clothes. I just told her I was going outside. She sat at the kitchen table.

When I returned after finishing the driveway, she was sitting in the same place. She asked who I was. I said, "If I told you, you wouldn't believe me."

She said, "You're my Jim."

I said, "Yes."

The rest of the day has been wonderful. She is still fearful of the other Jim Adams.

I remember how strange it was that I left the house being accused of using "Jim's" coat, but when I spent some time shoveling snow from the driveway and returned I was another person. When she said, "You're *my* Jim," I was overjoyed.

That day we worked in the kitchen together, watched TV together, and spent time reading together. I could even hug her. We both had a wonderful day, and I thanked God so much for that day.

Capgras Syndrome discovery

-- Wednesday, January 1, 2014 --

As I reflect on the past year it is frightening what has happened to Diane. She has gone from having slight balance and memory problems to not being able to cast a fishing line, not knowing where she is, not being married, not knowing me, always wanting to "go home," and having hallucinations and paranoia. This has happened since June 2013, a short six months.

Today the bad Jim Adams came back. It happened while we were watching a concert on Public Television, just out of the blue.

The grief caused by losing Diane to Lewy Body Dementia has been difficult. I know that in another six months this disease may cause a complete loss of the Diane I always knew. It's like going through a death in ultra slow motion. I just pray for a good year for Diane and for patience on my part so I can make life for her as pleasant as possible.

Having a background in aerospace engineering was perhaps a liability to me during this time. Engineers have to understand things, and when there are problems, they fix them. I was dealing with something that was incomprehensible and could not be fixed.

I needed to know what was causing Diane's condition and spent countless hours searching the Internet for causes of Lewy Body Dementia with Parkinson's Disease only to be frustrated by the fact that the cause was unknown. Only the symptoms and behaviors were known. This butted against my engineering mind-set and was hard for me to accept.

Knowing there was nothing I or the medical community could do to arrest or reverse the processes churning in Diane's brain was a major stress point with me. One of the things that was very evident in the research I did was that Diane's condition was terminal, that it was a matter of time before the diseases would take her life. I knew her condition would worsen over time, but that time span was unknown. My research told me it might be between 2 and 20 years with an average span of 5 to 7 years.

Diane did not want to linger in a state of mental incapacity and was particularly worried about becoming a burden to others. At this stage in the processes of the diseases I was thinking two scenarios: 1) things might progress as rapidly as they had during the past six months, or 2) Diane's condition might last for several years. I planned to give Diane all the love, care, and comfort I possibly could during her remaining time. All other things had to become secondary; this was THE mission for me. I wanted to be there for Diane every possible moment.

-- Thursday, January 2, 2014 --

I spent the time before Diane got up doing more Lewy Body researching. I found a good booklet from the Lewy Body Association and am going to order a copy and get some copies for the kids.

Diane wondered if it was OK to move her figurines to the other place in Chetek. I said, "OK, let's do it in the morning." We'll see if she remembers that.

Responding by saying, "Let's do it in the morning," seemed to work very well. Diane would accept this almost all the time. I don't recall her ever remembering the next morning that she needed to move things to "the other place." It is still hard to say things like this, knowing I am saying it just to redirect her.

-- Friday, January 3, 2014 --

Last night was a night from hell. Diane didn't know who I was or where she was. There was absolutely no way she would accept that we were married.

When we tried talking she stared in a distant gaze and would shake her head and roll her eyes at each question I tried to answer. She became very belligerent after I convinced her to not to go out in the cold to see her dad. She wouldn't go to bed with me but told me to "get my coat on and go." Finally, I got her to agree that I could sleep in the other bedroom.

I got my clothes and slept in the spare bedroom. I suspect that is how things will be from now on. Before Diane went to bed she was searching for her "little girl." She did not know who that was. A very Lewy Body night.

I spent two hours researching on the computer this morning. I sincerely believe Diane has a very classic case of Capgras Syndrome (pronounced "Cap-graw"). This happens when the visual and emotional connections in the brain are severed. This is why Diane sees more than one of me and views me as an imposter and why she believes we have more than one house in town. This is quite a rare syndrome; however, as I read about cases of people living with Capgras Syndrome, everything matches the behaviors I see in Diane.

It is difficult to understand Capgras Syndrome. Normally, when Diane looked at me, the image her eyes saw was sent to the brain's visual processing area. The brain automatically searched the emotional part of the brain to find pathways of emotional memories associated with that image. Emotional thoughts might be associated with our high school days, our love for each other, special times spent with each other, times of trials, happiness, my being a father to our children, etc. If the brain made associated pathway connections with its visual and emotional parts, it told Diane I was her husband, Jim.

Of course, all this happens in a matter of milliseconds each time we see something with our eyes. When there is no emotional memory associated with a particular image, be it a person or place, our brain tells us we are seeing a complete stranger or a strange place. The brain naturally causes us to be skeptical of people or places with which we have no previous experiences. That's a matter of survival.

There are millions of pathways the brain accesses to find visual and emotional connections. At times, Diane's brain might have followed a correct pathway. She would see me as "her Jim." If the pathways were blocked or damaged by Lewy Body excessive proteins, the brain failed to make any connections between its visual and emotional parts, Diane's brain then couldn't associate my image with any emotional memories. She saw "another Jim."

On the other hand, the pathways the brain uses may have connected the visual image with an emotion completely unassociated with the original image. The new pathway may be associated with negative emotions, creating the illusion that I was an imposter trying to harm her.

For similar reasons, Diane saw more than one house, and objects would appear to move instantaneously from one house to another, depending on which path the brain took to circumvent the Lewy Body blockage.

This is a cruel disease indeed.

What a terrible feeling Diane must experience: seeing me around the house constantly as an imposter and believing there is an identical house with identical belongings in identical places...UGH!

I'm hoping that Diane doesn't begin to see our kids as imposters. According to my reading this sometimes happens. Psychiatrists also suggest it's best to try to get into the Capgras patient's thought process and try to "shoo" away the imposter. It might work to take Diane out of the house and then return so she may see it as a familiar place.

Mel and Cleo, Diane's siblings, paid a surprise visit this afternoon. It was good for Diane to see them. We had a wonderful visit filled with fun and laughter. Diane got a few things mixed up, but she did quite well.

While working on a puzzle today, Diane said, "I guess I'll have to go." She put on her coat and gloves and started out the door. It is -10 degrees. I finally convinced her to stay here. She was going across the street to see her dad.

Diane went to bed about 8:30 PM, after some gentle persuasion. She apologized for my having to sleep in the "small" bed. Interesting.

-- Saturday, January 4, 2014 --

I made a batch of pumpkin bars. While I was working in the kitchen, Diane was reading this journal. She read the list of symptoms I had listed and about Capgras Syndrome. Sometime during the afternoon the Jim Adams that she was married to "came back." She asked questions for over an hour about her symptoms. Diane seemed to comprehend what I was saying and was concerned about the possibility of "walking off" somewhere. She went into our other bedroom and wondered why my pajamas and clothes were there. I explained her "fear of the other Jim Adams." She was so sorry that happened. She wanted me to sleep in our bed, and I did. I love her!

These times when Diane recognized me as her husband were precious. She wanted to know everything I could tell her about her condition. She asked questions like, "How did I get Lewy Body? How long have I had this? What will happen as time goes on? How long will it last? Is there a cure?" I answered each question as well as I could from the research I had done on the Internet. Diane looked at me when I spoke to her, and asked follow up questions. We had what seemed to me to be a very normal conversation. Her fears of not being able to control her behavior were logical and seemed very genuine.

The most difficult questions to answer concerned how long the disease would last and what would happen as time went on. Telling someone you love there is no cure for their terminal disease is an overwhelming task. I had to tell her that moving her limbs would become more difficult, her ability to recognize people and places would degrade, her brain would not be able to make logical connections, she might not be able to walk, her appetite would decrease, and it would become hard to swallow. Her physical body would simply cease to function.

As difficult as it was to talk about these things, Diane wanted to know what might happen. She told me she hoped it wouldn't last long and said, "I hope it comes quick." I couldn't help but admire her courage in the face of this formidable foe.

-- Monday, January 6, 2014 --

Diane is up at 7:30 AM which is quite early for her. This morning she is seeing "a girl from Luther Park Bible Camp." Diane went into the bedrooms and came back to tell me, "She is gone."

Throughout the entire day Diane was paranoid over "kids" being left out in the cold by themselves. "Kids" often means grandchildren or our own kids, as Diane has forgotten they are all grown up.

Tonight Capgras Syndrome was pretty extreme. This time it was "going home" to the other house. I finally relented and offered to get in the car and take her there. We proceeded to get our winter coats on, it's -15 degrees out, and Diane said, "I don't know the way." She finally gave in after a long time of trying (unsuccessfully) to convince her to stay here. She became very negative towards anything I said to answer her endless questions, and we both had to sit down and be quiet. She fell asleep in the recliner.

-- Tuesday, January 7, 2014 --

We have another -20 degree morning. All schools are closed for a second day. Right now at 7 AM it is peaceful and quiet. No continuous questions, paranoia regarding houses and payments, explanations about our kids being grown up, no "other Jim Adams." Just quiet-- wonderful.

This morning Diane was very upset because I had made the "kids" go out in the -20 degree cold to sort ice cream.

Capgras Syndrome really took over today. I'm not Jim Adams the husband, this isn't "home," this isn't our house, etc.

Tonight around 5 PM Diane wanted "outta here." We were putting our winter clothes on. I got the car started and backed out of the garage ready to try to find "home." Suddenly she said, "Can I call?"

"Call who?" I asked.

"Laurie," she said. "I can sleep on the floor."

I dialed Laurie, and Diane explained that she needed a place to sleep tonight. Laurie offered to come over. I told her that would be great. Laurie fixed dinner for us. I went for a ride so I was gone for a while. When I returned, Diane asked where I had been and if I had seen "that guy." I told her I got rid of him, told him to get out of our lives. That seemed to be OK with her.

Greg came over for a visit about 7 PM. Diane was pretty good but still wondered if she could get home. Don also called and talked with Diane a while. She told Don she was sitting with Greg and "Dad" (referring to me). She didn't see me while talking to Don.

Diane was very firm about wanting to "get out of here," and there was little I could do to get her mind off the subject. Sometimes she would push me or strike out at me when I offered to take her hand and lead her into the living room. I was so thankful that Laurie could come over to help Diane. Diane always seems to settle down and change her mind about "getting out of here" after talking with either Greg or Laurie. Having one of them come to the house to help get Diane settled down was becoming quite regular.

The delusion of some criminal organization trying to take over the house, etc., was particularly strong today.

While we were working on the puzzle today Diane asked if I was going to kill her. One day she asked me if I was going to kill the kids.

I think the delusion of my belonging to a criminal organization trying to take over the house caused Diane to feel like I was a gangster. She would ask me about killing her or the kids in a sort of "casual" language, never seeming to be afraid of me. She would just keep working on the puzzle as if my answer, "I would never think of doing such a thing," was a normal part of conversation. Such conversations always bring me back to the thought, "It is not Diane, it is the Lewy Body Dementia."

Tonight Diane wanted me to sleep in our bed because she felt safer with me there.

89

It was extremely difficult to know how to handle sleeping arrangements. I was so concerned about Diane waking up in the morning from a scary dream and finding me, the "imposter Jim," with her in bed. Other times she would want me to sleep in our bed because she would be afraid if I didn't. This was a daily struggle.

-- Wednesday, January 8, 2014 --

Diane walked in this morning wondering where everyone went. I told her I didn't know. She went back to bed and fell asleep again.

Diane was very "moody" this morning. She was angry with me for letting the kids jump on the bed and turn the lights on and off.

Prior to Lewy Body Dementia, Diane seldom told me of any dreams she had during the night. She suddenly begin telling me about what she had experienced. These "dreams" were so real to her that she actually woke up from the perceived movement or visual images.

During late afternoon, after we went for a short ride around Chetek, Diane was paranoid over a funeral. Our house is the funeral parlor that is making the arrangements. She was wondering if Norma and Cleo were doing anything. It got bad enough that Diane called Cleo around 8:30 PM and wanted to know if she was coming up for the funeral. Of course this caught Cleo completely off guard. I talked to Cleo before Diane hung up the phone and explained what was happening.

Cleo was very gracious about Diane calling. I apologized for the call and explained to Cleo that Diane insisted on calling. Cleo understood completely and was surprised by how fast her sister's dementia was progressing. Cleo assured me it didn't matter when Diane called, she would talk to her. This is another example of the wonderful support Diane's siblings provided.

-- Thursday, January 9, 2014 --

This morning our bedroom was "being painted," and a moment later Diane said our bedroom was a hospital. She did go back to sleep around 7:15 AM.
Chris arrived at 7:30 AM, and it was still below zero. Little Gwen and Reuben were in their pajamas, but Gwen was ready to start playing with the toys. Diane got up just before I left for Cameron High School to do some volunteering. She was a little light-headed, so Chris kept an eye on her as she got ready for the day.

Greg stayed with Diane for dinner, and Laurie, Addy and I went to Rice Lake to watch our grandson Taylor swim at the pool there.

It was SO VERY GOOD to have gotten away for a day.

Helping out at the school in Cameron was a welcome break. Having conversations with high school age students was a treat; no other Jim's, no nonexistent funerals, just normal conversation. Being able to watch Taylor swim was a pleasure. The caregiver classes emphasized the importance of taking care of ourselves and this was an example of that. I remember how refreshed I felt after a day away from my caretaker role.

-- Friday, January 10, 2014 --

This is a paranoia morning. Diane and I do not own our house. She will not accept that it is ours. So I must just refer to the house as a place to stay, not "our" place to stay.

Today's Capgras Syndrome revolved around getting all our "stuff" moved to the "other place" in time.

Diane was also worried about her brother Roger, wondering where he was. It seemed to be OK with her if I explained Roger has his own apartment in Galesville, Wisconsin.

Diane's brother Roger

-- Saturday, January 11, 2014 --

In late afternoon the Capgras Syndrome really kicked in. This time she wanted to go to the "other house." It got bad enough that we actually walked up and down the street to try and find the "other house." When we reached the west end of the block, and Diane didn't see the "other house," she said I had moved it. (Lewy Body speaking here.)

When we got back to our house, I asked Diane if she recognized the place. She said she recognized the garage but wasn't sure about the house.

I'm sure the neighbors thought we were both crazy. It was the middle of January, late in the afternoon, and we were going for a walk dressed up in our winter gear. Diane didn't seem to be bothered by the cold. She held on to me during the entire walk for fear of falling or slipping on the snow-covered road. This was one of the first times I noticed how slowly and deliberately she was walking. It wasn't because of the snow on the road, it was just how she had to walk. Her mobility was certainly getting worse.

I asked her to let me know when she saw the "other house." There are only two other houses between our house and the end of the block. When we got to the end of the block, Diane stopped, looked around for a while and told me I must have moved the house. She couldn't see it. Capgras Syndrome is so strange!

This evening Diane had to call Greg and Chris to let them know she needed a ride home. She was at a place called Daybreak and needed to be "picked up." Chris was home, and convinced Diane I was trustworthy and she should get some sleep. I slept in the other bed again tonight. I don't dare completely move into the other bedroom either because sometimes Diane doesn't want that.

-- Sunday, January 12, 2014 --

As I was getting the computer hooked up to our TV, Diane came in and said, "Still here, huh?" As we talked I knew that the imposter Jim Adams was alive and well.

We had the same, "Guess I'll go home now," battle tonight. I convinced Diane to stay here. She finally agreed it was alright, as long as I slept in the other bedroom. I think this will be an everyday thing soon.

-- Monday, January 13, 2014 --

Things were pretty good early in the day. Mid-afternoon we took a trip to the post office. The weather was sunny and mild, so we drove on CTY HWY M north of town and ended up in Cameron. Diane was insistent about going "home." She also wanted to find my "place of business" in town (a tavern) where "the two girls" in our house work. Diane thinks it is a pretty shady business and the police should be involved.

First we tried to drive around Chetek to find "home." The first place we stopped was Greg and Laurie's house. Diane insisted it was her brother Melvin's house. When we passed it again it was her mom and dad's, then it was Cleo's when we stopped at the stop sign. We drove through town never finding the "business" she was looking for.

Diane did lead me to our actual house, and we parked in the driveway just in front of the garage. I asked her if she recognized the house. Diane said it was her folks' home. She didn't know how her dad would accept me. I reminded her that her folks had passed away many years ago. She seemed to accept that. I explained to her that I was "her Jim." She didn't want to go in the house. She waited by the steps as I parked the car and unlocked the house. Diane couldn't figure out why I would have a key.

As we talked she seemed to accept for a while that I was "her Jim." I even got to put my arms around her and give her a hug!

When I was able to give Diane a hug, she would hold me tight for a long time. This was another way I knew she saw me as "her Jim." I had to be careful to give her hugs only when I believed she saw me as her Jim. If I was wrong, and that happened many times, she would shove me away. Even though I knew it was Lewy Body Dementia, that rejection was always difficult to accept.

-- Tuesday, January 14, 2014 --

As I came out of the bathroom this morning, Diane was coming down the hall with her clothes, ready to shower. I asked her if she was still tired. She said she was. I convinced her to return to bed and rest some more. Her words to me as I tucked her in were, "I need a ride home when I wake up." UGH!

I am trying to foil Lewy Body as best I can. According to Diane, I'm still "someone else" who seems to be managing this housing complex and is possibly involved in some kind of illegal operation. The best way I've found to handle this situation is to speak as little as possible and answer the relentless questions with vague answers or not answer at all, saying, "I have no clue."

Sometimes I could simply say, "It's Lewy, Diane," and we both knew what that meant. Often she would literally drill me--and I mean like a lawyer--on my involvement in "illegal operations" at the housing complex we were living in. Diane would have made a great detective or lawyer at times like these. Her questioning was relentless, and her mind persevered. I could "play along" for quite a while; however, there always came a point when I could no longer answer questions. She simply stumped me. I couldn't think fast enough. When I reached the "I have no clue" point, we both had to stop the conversation and be quiet.

I went out to blow the snow off the driveway. When I returned I was Diane's Jim. Go figure! It's an example of the lack of emotional and visual brain communication.

Things went well until it was time for bed. We had to go through the "I want to go home" struggle. It's getting harder to win this battle each day.

-- Wednesday, January 15, 2014 --

Diane has seen me as her Jim all day--what a relief. At bedtime she wanted me to sleep in our bed. She even wondered where my pillow was. However, after she finished in the bathroom, she came out and told me she had changed her mind.

-- Thursday, January 16, 2014 --

I got up right at the alarm today at 5:30 AM. It is excellent to have quiet time without the constant wondering where "they" went, answering questions that I have to wonder which "Jim" is being addressed, having to try to convince someone, "This is home...."

I noticed a handwritten note on the counter where Diane had written the words "Lewe Body 5 PM w/DEBBRA SEPX$_E^E$T NP." The writing is very uneven and the letters are not well formed. This is the first I've seen her write since before Christmas.

Diane had stopped journaling well before Christmas when her handwriting was still quite good. This note revealed a startling change. The date was incorrect, letters were very uneven and nonsensical, uppercase and lowercase mixed and lines very uneven. This little note made it abundantly clear just how fast the disease was progressing. I remember being afraid, not knowing just how long Diane would be with me.

This afternoon Diane couldn't remember our children's names or where they lived.

-- Friday, January 17, 2014 --

Diane came in the kitchen as I was taking down the window coverings. I asked if she slept well last night. She said, "No, there were a bunch of kids all over." I convinced her to go back to bed and sleep some more, as there was nothing going on this morning.

The paranoia today is over getting everyone "shots" at the clinic. It lasted the better part of the day. Diane gets agitated and worried that the kids won't get their shots.

We went out to eat with Greg, Laurie, and Addy around 5:45 PM and met Laurie's cousin and her husband at the restaurant. Before we left the restaurant Diane asked me if the sleeping arrangements had been made. She wanted to know where each of us was sleeping (me and her). She accepted that our house was "home" tonight.

Diane did very well during the meal. She listened to our conversations and responded to my questions about the food and how it tasted. But she kept asking me about the arrangements. She was talking about the arrangements for our living together and not being married. I would tell her everything was arranged and not to worry. Laurie understood what was happening and talked with Diane as Greg and I went out to the car. She convinced Diane that I was sleeping separate from her, and our house was an okay place to stay that night.

Other Jims, other houses and a serious fall

-- Monday, January 20, 2014 --

Long night. Diane woke up to use the bathroom at 2:30 AM and went back to bed after checking to see what was happening in my room. She awoke again at 4:14 AM wondering what was happening "with the kids." She went back to bed but got up and sat in her bedroom chair while I got ready. She was totally incoherent, talking about school, deep snow, getting Addy to school, calling the Cameron Superintendent ("Mr. Jerdet"--no such person), etc. I convinced her to get some more sleep. She went back to bed but wanted to know if "the message" she sent to her dad got through. She finally went back to sleep.

There was no coherence to anything Diane said or did today. She has been seeing all kinds of things--kids, old people, rats, you name it. Our house is at times a church camp, a lawyer's office, or a rental house. Today is the most irrational I've seen Diane yet.

I moved my clothes from my dresser to the other bedroom this evening.

Today seems to be a huge leap in the severity of Lewy Body/Capgras Syndrome. I think Lewy Body Dementia is causing Diane to become more apathetic as time goes on.

This was the first time an entire day was chaotic. There were always "down times" when Diane would sleep or just sit in her "comfy" chair and look at a magazine. But things were starting to change. The hallucinations, illusions, and delusions were more continuous during the time Diane was awake. I could satisfy her question about "the message" she sent to her dad by saying, "I think so, but I'll check again." However, I was getting less and less effective at satisfying her mind.

-- Tuesday, January 21, 2014 --

Yes, a good night's sleep for both of us.

When Diane is awake there seems to be little or no relation to the "now" world. Today Lewy Body has her in a church camp. We are responsible for all the kids, getting busses arranged, and organizing activities. For example, this afternoon as we were eating she heard a presenter upstairs speaking to a large group.

There is a smile once in awhile, but Diane displays little visible emotion.

Today, I also noticed pronounced tremors as Diane put a glass to her mouth to drink juice.

I knew that tremors were a symptom of Parkinson's Disease but hadn't noticed any until this incident. Her hand began to shake very slightly but enough to cause the juice to ripple in the glass. Witnessing the arrival of this symptom gave me a sinking feeling in my stomach. The Parkinson's Disease symptoms were beginning to accelerate.

-- Wednesday, January 22, 2014 --

Diane was pretty good during the day. The Capgras Syndrome reared its ugly head again close to bedtime. Within just a few minutes I went from "her Jim" to the "other Jim" while sitting right beside her.

The transition from her Jim to another Jim might happen when I left the room and returned. It might happen when we were sitting beside each other, or it might happen when she was looking directly at me. It seemed to happen more often when we were with each other for extended periods of time. There were clues that I had transitioned from one Jim to another. For example, Diane might say, "Where did you come from?" or "It's you again," or "You're my Jim." Other times, there was no indication, and I didn't know which Jim I was.

Not knowing was the hardest part. I didn't know which point of view to use in a conversation. I had to wait to see which Jim I was. How Diane's brain could recognize me and inform me which Jim she was seeing was always a mystery to me and kept me on my toes.

As I was putting the breakfast dishes into the dishwasher, Diane looked at me for a long time and said, "You really are my Jim." I said yes, and gave her a big hug. Thank God for small moments like this.

Diane is still in a camp/school/church setting, always worried about the little kids. I'm usually able to satisfy her concerns by telling her the bus has taken them to school or the children were picked up by their parents.

The literature on working with dementia often mentions "getting into the mind" of the person afflicted. When Diane appeared to be in a given setting, such as a school, we could have a conversation as long as I could put myself in the time, place, and situation she seemed to be experiencing. By imagining what she might be seeing and thinking, we could have a reasonable conversation. It was actually very rewarding to be able to have a several minute conversation with Diane, even though it was imaginary. In a small way, I felt we were together again.

This evening Diane opened the door--it is cold outside--and called to the "kids" to come in where it is warm. She gets so confused trying to see out of our window, which has small areas of flat glass surrounded by tapered frames like prisms. It's ironic that when we bought the door, I wanted clear glass but Diane wanted the prism type because it was more private.

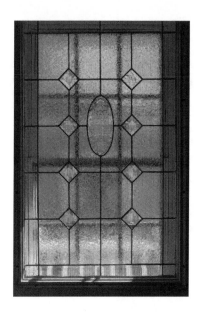

Our entry door that gave Diane such frustration

-- Friday, January 24, 2014 --

I practiced banjo this morning--what a joy. I haven't been able to practice for three days.

Diane again had the idea that I have three brothers (I only have one, a twin). We are having a "discussion" and my three brothers suddenly turned into turtles.

We played Yahtzee this afternoon. It is very difficult for her to choose which dice to keep and remember how many times she has shaken the dice. I don't think she enjoyed playing. There was no excitement or emotion, even when shaking four sixes at once.

-- Saturday, January 25, 2014 --

I was preparing breakfast this morning and watched Diane walk into the kitchen area. I noticed just how slow and shuffling her walk was. She moved like she wasn't sure about her balance.

When I was with Diane every day, the small changes in her walking weren't noticeable. It takes a moment of reflection comparing what "used to be" with "now" to realize just how much things change. Diane was taking very small steps, more like shuffling. Here is another Parkinson's symptom I knew about but had never realized was prevalent until I purposely observed her movement. The wait for these symptoms to appear was always in my mind, but they happened so slowly I didn't realize their progression.

Often Diane strolls around the house examining places and objects. I'm sure she is seeing things due to shadows and colors.

She came up to me and whispered into my ear that she wanted to show me something. She took me into her bedroom and pointed to the bedside stand to show me the "bugs" that were there and also on the bedspread. Of course, they weren't there. "They always go away when I want to show somebody," she said.

There is more talk involving her mom and dad and what they will think of our "living together" and not being married. There is also a lot of concern for Cleo, Norma, and Roger, her siblings.

-- Monday, January 27, 2014 --

Capgras Syndrome was bad this afternoon: two or more Jims and two houses. It was relentless. I again had to leave the room in hopes that upon returning I might be "her Jim" again. That never happened.

About 9:00 PM, as I was reading, Diane came in my bedroom and carefully looked in the nooks and crannies of the room to see if "the kids" were there. She just turned around and went back to her bedroom. A little while later she came into the bedroom again and asked where the kids were. I said they were just fine.
A few minutes after I began reading again, I heard this awful thump/bang. I rushed into Diane's bedroom. It was dark. I turned on the light and saw her lying on the floor by the west window. She was on her side and a little propped up. I went over and hugged her and asked if she hurt anywhere. I noticed blood on the carpet. I lifted her up and sat her on the bed. I couldn't see any blood on her face or

body. Finally she put her hand up to her head, and her finger had blood on it. She had a fairly deep cut in the left side of her head just above the ear. I rushed to get some wet washcloths and Kleenex. The wound kept bleeding and was quite deep. We put on her clothes and went to the emergency room at the Barron Hospital. They measured the wound to be about two centimeters and put four staples in to close it. She also got a Tetanus shot just to be sure. The emergency personnel were wonderful.

Diane said she must have blacked out getting into bed. I'm thinking, since it was dark in the room, she might have thought she was getting into bed and fell because the bed wasn't there. She must have been totally disoriented.

This could have been much worse. She put a dent in the floor radiator, so she must have hit very hard. This is Diane's fourth fall.

The feeling I had when I turned on the light and saw Diane on the floor after this fall is one I never want to experience again. I was torn between being mad at myself for not being able to stop something like this and shear panic trying to think of what to do to help her.

-- Tuesday, January 28, 2014 --

Laurie texted me this morning wondering if things were OK. I sent a text back telling her of our visit to the emergency room. She will come over and help Diane clean her hair.

Last night was very scary. This is the fourth fall since August. But this one resulted in real injury. It's impossible to be there every time Diane moves. This happened just a few feet from where I was in bed reading.

I couldn't help feeling guilty about the fall. It happened in the house. I was responsible for her care. I kept wondering what I could have done differently to prevent such a fall. I still wonder about these things.

Diane slept most of the day. When she woke up the Capgras Syndrome was severe. After dinner she called Greg to let him know she had a "problem." Greg came over and had a talk for a while. Diane thought

102

he also was part of a scam and "in on everything." He was able to convince her to stay here and that I was an "OK guy" to stay here with her.

Diane didn't remember who took care of her when she fell last night. At first it was one of the boys I had in school, and then she didn't know. She thinks there were two people who took her to Barron and then they just went away. How did she get home? She didn't know.

I'm not sure how long I can do this.

-- Wednesday, January 29, 2014 --

Kip, our neighbor across the street, came over and was wondering if all was OK, as they had seen us leave the house at 10:30 PM on Monday. They thought it was strange to see us leave when it was fifteen below zero. He wanted me to call anytime I needed help. What wonderful neighbors.

I noticed this morning, that there was a large black and blue area in the middle of Diane's back. She must have hit her back on the chair or the chest of drawers. She said there was no pain.

I spent almost all afternoon convincing Diane that I was her caregiver, and her children wanted her to stay here in this house so she was safe and they (the children) didn't have to worry about her. It worked well enough that she went to bed without the normal "I want to walk home" struggle.

-- Thursday, January 30, 2014 --

I walked behind Diane down the hall to her bedroom. I notice that she staggered right and left, actually touching the wall to keep her balance.

We seem to be in some "care center" most of the time now. I'm the caregiver, and the children have chosen this place for her to stay because of her illness. It's working so far.

Diane spent more than two hours sorting and changing purses this afternoon. She has combined her ostomy changing supplies with her purse contents in a black canvas bag.

As she came away from reorganizing her purses, Diane said she felt like she was going to throw up. We made it to the kitchen sink and she threw up. There was nothing but clear mucus coming up. I asked her how long she had felt like this, and she said a couple of days. How do you know what to believe when there is no concept of time?

I had no clue Diane was not feeling well. My thoughts at the time were that she might be feeling some dizziness, particularly after watching her walk down the hall that morning. I don't know if the brain trying to find connections can cause a sense of sickness, but this seemed unusual. I wondered also if there was some effect from her fall. It's so difficult, in most cases impossible, to understand the brain's antics when dementia is present.

An Angry Diane

A REALLY BAD DAY

I got up at 5:30 AM. When I came out of the bathroom, Diane was standing in the doorway to my room and startled me. She said she wasn't supposed to be here, and she had fallen last night at home while going upstairs. She insisted she wasn't supposed to be here. I finally convinced her to go back to bed, saying her children wanted her in this place. As I tucked her in, she said that Cleo and Norma needed to be called. I told her we had a phone chain, and they knew about the fall.

This afternoon we were going to take a trip to the bank and stores in Chetek and Cameron. But when I wanted to get the checkbook out of Diane's purse, she went "ballistic." She swore at me for stealing funds from her account. I tried to calm her down by saying that her children wanted me to manage the checkbook. I also explained that because of her illness she couldn't do the math anymore. We both began to cry. I couldn't take seeing her in this state. She called Greg, and he stopped in when he got home from school. He convinced her to trust her caregiver.

I finally convinced Diane to allow me to manage the checkbook. It is no longer in Diane's purse. I put it in a drawer downstairs, so I can use it when managing our finances.

In our 50-plus years of marriage, I had never observed Diane angry. We had never had a disagreement in which either of us got so angry we shouted or swore. But the anger Diane showed over the checkbook was severe. I could *see* the anger on her face and in her eyes. I can safely say I know what anyone who is verbally abused must feel like. The swearing and accusations just kept coming out of her mouth in rapid succession. I remember wanting to flee the house. It took everything I had in me to stay with her.

When something like this happens, the first thing that comes to your mind is not, "Oh it's the Lewy Body Dementia." The first instinct is to react as you would in normal circumstances. I immediately felt a deep pang, much like I felt when my dad or mom scolded me as a child. But this coming from the one I deeply loved was physically hurtful. I felt sick to my stomach.

There were two people during this incident that needed calming down. First, I needed to calm myself, and then I needed to calm Diane. When I explained she couldn't do the checkbook anymore due to the Lewy Body Dementia, and that her children wanted me to handle the finances, she stopped her rage. Diane began to cry. It was in such opposition to her anger that I too began to cry.

-- Saturday, February 1, 2014 --

It's about 7:00 AM, cloudy and cold today. Diane needs to wash her head wound today. I'll help her if she will let me.

Earlier in the day Diane talked on the phone to her sister Norma. She did pretty well, but I'm sure Norma didn't understand some things Diane was asking/talking about.

Diane's sister Norma

While sitting together watching TV and answering the always present questions, Diane said, "What are you talking about?" Suddenly I was "her Jim," her husband. She even said, "I love you," as she went to bed.

"Her Jim" hasn't been around for at least a week. A moment of real JOY!

When we were sitting in our living room watching TV, Diane would often start asking questions, usually clarification questions regarding the place in which she thought we were living or people she thought were in our house. This conversation seemed to be going along a normal Lewy Body routine. As I tried to answer a question, without any hesitation, Diane just said, "Where did you come from?" We had been sitting together for quite some time so it surprised me. When I asked who I was, she immediately replied, "My Jim." It was like returning from one of my long trips while working for NASA or the Air Force and seeing Diane again. The times when "her Jim" was in her mind were becoming rare.

-- Monday, February 3, 2014 --

I noticed Diane had put two rolls of toilet paper out, one on the stool top and one on top of the paper cup dispenser. It's getting hard to keep track of where things are like her purse, kitchen utensils, her ostomy supplies, etc. I had to put Greg and Laurie's house key in the locked medicine box because it kept getting lost. I once found it in her ostomy purse.

The misplacement of things is something I learned to live with. If I observed Diane putting an item somewhere unusual I would try to remember where she put it. Sometimes I would retrieve the item and put it in its normal place while Diane was sleeping. I don't recall her ever missing an object she had misplaced.

I'm actually still finding surprises as I open drawers or closets these days. To me it is a "loving" reminder that Diane was here. I always smile when recovering one of these "misplaced" items from a strange location.

It's really difficult to drive our car with Diane along. She seems to remember it is our car but really gets mad because "her Jim" is not driving the car. I shouldn't "be allowed to drive the car anytime I want."

It bothered Diane a lot that I would drive or use the computer any time I wanted. She would tell me, "That computer belongs to Dad," or "Only Jim should be driving the car." I was careful to let her know I was going to use the car or computer, and sometimes, depending on the dementia at the time, I found it easier to ask her permission to use the computer or car.

-- Tuesday, February 4, 2014 --

Diane is confused about the next doctor appointment. Reading the calendar is next to impossible; couple this with the paranoia of missing the appointment, and it is difficult to watch.

Today it seems that Diane's mind is going back in time. Our kids are 9 or 10 years old and there is paranoia over their being left alone at night. At one point I asked her who I was, and she told me I was her son.

I texted and talked with Don tonight. He, Chris, and Heidi, toured a memory care center in Eau Claire. They were pretty impressed with the facilities. Don said the head person there was surprised at how fast Diane's dementia was progressing. Well, she isn't the only one.

Being able to have the kids visit various memory care facilities was a relief. They all loved Diane so much, I knew they would find an excellent place for her. This was the first of several they checked out. We wanted to find a place that was familiar with Lewy Body Dementia with Parkinson's Disease. Thankfully, most were.

-- Wednesday, February 5, 2014 --

Diane was up at around 5:30 AM to use the bathroom. She seemed to handle turning the lights on OK. Last night when we were walking to her bedroom, the nightlight on the floor outlet turned on automatically as we passed. Diane immediately tried to step over the light beam as if it were an obstacle.

Tonight, Diane's mind has been jumping all over the place: worried about Addy, then Mabel (who has been dead for years), then Cleo's sister-in-law, then worried about someone coming into the house with a gun. It's been a mentally exhausting two and a half hours.

Diane has been very agitated tonight. She is wondering "what to do," wanting to go home, wringing her hands and walking back and forth. She lashed out at me over the car keys. Just out of the blue the keys became an issue. UGH!

The lashing out was becoming common. It always took a little time for me to adjust to the idea that it wasn't Diane, it was Lewy Body. What made it particularly difficult was the lashing out was random, with no clues or prompting.

-- Thursday, February 6, 2014 --

The event for the day is getting the staples removed from Diane's head wound. Diane regularly doesn't know the day, month or year. Time is a real problem for her. She can't understand why the clock keeps "jumping around" all the time. Sometimes she looks at the digital clock and sees 10 PM when it is 7 PM, or she will ask the time and think it is morning when it is night and vice versa.

We went to the clinic about 2 PM and had Diane's staples taken out. Diane has been in a different place today. To her Cleo and Norma have been here, off and on, all day. It's like she doesn't remember from minute to minute. Most of the afternoon she thought I was her dad. Then she would wonder where her dad was even when I was standing beside her.

TONIGHT, WOW!

I was sitting in the living room with Diane. It was about 8 PM. We were having "normal" conversations about people coming and going in "the place." I hesitate to use the word "house," as to Diane this is a church, school, or caregiving place of some kind.

We decided to go to bed. I went downstairs to read emails and shut the computer down. I thought Diane went to bed; however, after a few minutes she came down the basement steps. Diane stopped short of coming all the way down and said, "I'm sorry but I'm going to have to ask you to leave!" I calmly asked why she would ask me to leave. The answer was that I was not to be on her dad's computer, it was one of his private things. (Her dad passed away in 1968 at the age of 62.) She was tired of me "coming in and taking over the place." I could not convince Diane that I was her caregiver and the children wanted her in this house to keep her safe.

She got her cell phone and was going to call her sister Cleo to tell her about the "situation," as she put it. She got Greg on the phone, not Cleo, thank goodness. She told Greg she didn't want me around anymore. "He just takes over the place and treats me like a child." Greg came to the house. She started to cry, and Greg went to her and held her. Bless him. After awhile he convinced her that I was OK, that I "came with the house."

After Greg left she got our "Adams-Nelson Story" book out and realized her dad had passed away, but she was still wondering where he is.

I knew I was in trouble. I followed Diane back up the stairs where she found her cell phone on the kitchen counter. I didn't want her to call Cleo, but there was nothing I could do or say to stop her from doing that. I had set her phone up to dial by names, so to call Cleo all she had to do was highlight "Cleo" on the list, press "Send," and it would dial for her. Fortunately, when she moved the cursor down on the phone she hit Greg's name instead of Cleo's.

After the phone conversation with Greg and while he was on his way to our house, Diane and I sat in our living room. She was on our couch, and I sat in one of the chairs opposite her. We didn't say anything. I was afraid I might upset her. I didn't know who she thought I was.

When Greg got to the house, Diane began to cry. His conversation with Diane reminded me of a father comforting a child upset at being away from home for the first time. Greg explained how he, Don, and Chris wanted her to be in "this place" so they didn't have to worry about her safety. The novel idea that I "came with the house" seemed to be okay with her.

It was very uncomfortable sitting across from them during this time. I remember asking myself, "Am I a husband, a caregiver, a father, or what?"

A visit to the doctor and a moment of reality

-- Friday, February 7, 2014 --

I feel emotionally drained after last night. It's getting to be a regular thing for Greg or Laurie to come here to get Diane settled down. This shouldn't have to be, and can't continue; they have their lives to live also.

Lewy Body Dementia makes Diane not know who I am, not trust me, not know where home is, live in other time periods, see other people and objects, and exhibit a host of other strange behaviors.

We have a 5 PM appointment with our doctor's assistant at the Rice Lake clinic today. I sent a letter updating them on Diane's condition. They are unable to spend much one-on-one time. Hopefully, the letter helps inform them of her condition.

Below is the letter sent to our doctor and assistant:

Here is an update on observed symptoms for Diane (since the last visit in November 2013). I hope this might help for our next visit on February 7, 2014.

Place and time: I don't think Diane knows from day to day where she is. Sometimes it's Colorado where we lived for eight years. Our house, to her, is some kind of Bible camp or scout camp where people are always coming and going, a funeral home, a hospital; once in awhile, when she asks, I'll tell her we live in Chetek, Wisconsin, and she will acknowledge that. There is no correlation of time and date. She often wonders why the clocks "jump" ahead or back in time. Dates on the calendar are almost impossible for her to figure out. She rarely knows what day it is.

Hallucinations: These continue about the same. She is taking the Rivastigmine, but it is very difficult to know if that helps since there is no real baseline to start with. She regularly sees other people in the house, sometimes family members, other times high school kids, scouts, and sometimes the "other Jim Adamses" (more on this later). She sometimes sees little and big bugs on a table or couch.

Visual interpretations: Diane is having more difficulty recognizing common objects. She will see the three mail boxes visible out our back window as three little girls, and these little girls are moving. Shadows and reflections are still a problem, and I've noticed little change in her reactions to these. Covering reflective surfaces that give her problems in the evening has helped.

Parkinsonism: I've noticed several things that are different from the last visit. Her walking gait is very slow and becoming more of a shuffle. There have been several instances of her stopping and waiting in one place because of balance – it doesn't seem to be dizziness but her sense of balance. Her posture is becoming more stooped, and coordination is difficult for fine motor skills using the hands. I've noticed an increase in tremors of the hand, particularly when holding a glass up to her mouth and also when holding a book. Her handwriting continues to degrade, and printing is almost impossible. However, normal handwriting is still fairly good. (See samples below.) There are continued problems trying to find the words she wants to use when speaking. On the evening of January 27, 2014, she fell in her bedroom, hitting her head on the floor heat register causing a trip to the emergency room at Barron Hospital. The result was a 2 cm wound on the left side of her head just above the ear.

REM sleep: There is an increase in the amount of body movements, twitching of hands and feet, and mouth movements. Once in awhile she will talk or make a screaming type of noise when she is asleep.

Depression: This remains about the same as last visit. She gets anxious when she can't understand why things are happening the way they are or why she is acting like she is. Diane will sometimes say she should just go off and die because she doesn't want to be a burden to others. She doesn't care much about anything in the "real world." She does get agitated sometimes when she can't "go home," but I'm usually successful at getting her to go to bed at night. She has tried to leave the house to "go home" a couple of times, but after she got her winter clothes on, she realized it was too cold to go out and was willing to sleep in her bed at the house.

Paranoia: This is now highly present. She is constantly very paranoid about our house mortgage papers being legal, about the kids and grandkids being OK and out of the cold, about kids catching the bus in the morning, and about people getting at our personal papers/possessions.

Capgras Syndrome: This is new since the last visit. To Diane there are two or more of me, "Jim Adams." One of them is "her Jim" and the other is a person involved in an organization that scams people. We are identical in appearance, wear the same clothes, but she wonders how the "bad" Jim knows so much about her and her family; she believes he has read and memorized everything about her past life and is able to recall anything she asks about – like a spy. Lately, there is even a third "Jim Adams" who is my brother. There are a lot of delusions involved with this syndrome involving "the scam" and people trying to take the house from us. The changing from one "Jim" to another is pretty random, and this makes it very difficult to try to communicate – wondering which "Jim" I am in the present. I often leave the room because things become so tense.

In addition, there are two or more houses she lives in. There is constant worry about getting things out of our house and moved to the "other place," which is on a hill. Often she will want to go to the other place but can't find it when we go for a walk or drive looking for it.

Physical health: Diane doesn't eat very much. She has little appetite. She does eat a balanced diet but servings are small. I can tell she has lost weight, but she is very happy with the weight loss saying, "I always wanted to be thin." We exercise on the treadmill regularly, and she does about ten minutes of slow walking while I use the exercise bike. I regularly ask her how she feels, and she seems to feel normal – no pain or abnormal issues. She often sleeps for long periods of time in the morning or afternoon. This has been normal for at least a year or possibly two. She is doing well with personal hygiene, showering, etc. She is able to change her ostomy bag, but it takes her much longer than

114

it used to. She did have a "mess" as she put it when she recently emptied her bag.

Issues to discuss at our next session:

What are the processes for getting help at the house when it will be needed?

Help with ostomy issues
Breaks for the caregiver – she is very reluctant to attend the adult day care
Insurance/Medicare help – what is required from clinic?
How do we determine when/if Diane is unable to care for herself?
How much is expected of home care?
When do we say, "Enough, Diane needs special care"?

Support:

I'm planning to attend the Lewy Body support group in Eau Claire, along with one or more of my children, as soon as the weather permits. I think this will help all of us.

I'm constantly reading about dementia and how to handle it. I'm currently reading *Creating Moments of Joy,* by Brackey. It's excellent.

I'm able to play banjo/guitar/harmonica and work on model airplanes to get breaks. I feel that I'm doing OK as a caregiver. I can get breaks when Diane is getting ready in the morning or when napping.

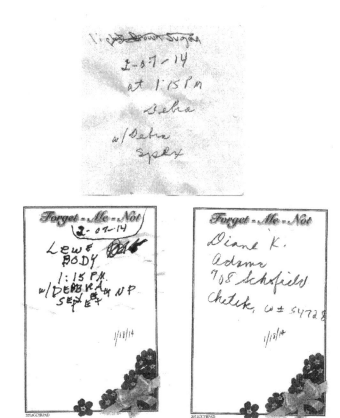

Sample handwriting for Diane January 2014

I find lying is hard on the brain even if it's to "help" one with dementia. If I don't say the right words it could set Diane off in an unknown direction. If that happens, I have to lie again to either redirect her or to see if I can have a conversation. If I were to describe what it is like living with and caring for a person with serious dementia it would be, "Constantly having to lie to live."

Sometimes, after trying to "get inside" Diane's head, my brain felt exhausted. The mental strain of trying to relate to someone with dementia was amplified by the idea that lying becomes a part of caregiving. There was the ever-present conflict between my moral value of not lying, and lying to help Diane in some way. As time went on this conflict was tempered by thinking of myself as an actor in a play.

116

It's 9 AM, Diane just came in the kitchen as I'm writing this journal entry. She wondered what the procedures were since this was her first time here. She wondered why my eyes looked red this morning. I told her I had a bad night. She said she didn't treat me very nice last night. At least she remembered something from last night.

Doctor's office notes:

Memory tests and drawing tests:

> *clock and time hand placement did OK*
> *3 words remembered 1 word*

Get on Barron County Office of Aging website for services

Start touring care centers

Palliative care should be checked out

Books: **Parkinson's Disease** *by Paul Tuite, MD*

Diane had a hard time going to bed tonight, insisting on going home. I finally convinced her we would see about tomorrow, but for now, her children want her here in this house for safety reasons.

Diane had to throw up again tonight as she was going to bed. She just threw up clear fluid like dry heaves.

-- Saturday, February 8, 2014 --

I feel a little better emotionally today. We will start the two Rivastigmine tablets at dinner today. I think we might try a 4:30 PM dosage and see how that works. Too close to bedtime and Diane may have severe nightmares.

Diane greeted me this morning with, "Are you still here?" She couldn't remember how to change her ostomy pouch, so we got out the instructions that came with the pouches. Once she got into the

117

bathroom, and I helped her lay everything out, she remembered how to do it.

Around 8:00 PM tonight while we were watching the Olympics, I turned around to see how Diane was doing. She said, "Where did you come from?" I looked at her and immediately asked if I was "her Jim." She said, "Yes!" That's the first time in at least a week that her Jim has been here. She wanted to know what was going on with her, why she was experiencing such weird things. We had a long conversation about Lewy Body Dementia and Parkinson's Disease. She expressed her feelings about not being a burden to the family. I told her she would never be a burden to any family member. Diane wondered why the family was being so good to her. I said, "Because you are loved very much." That seemed to have a real impact on her. She wondered about the time when she needed to go to a home. I explained that we all hoped that would be a long time yet, but the family was exploring possible homes. She seemed to be relieved that the kids were involved in the search for a good home.

This is the most intelligent and somewhat logical conversation we have had for many weeks. SUPER!

It was interesting that Diane was fully aware that something weird was happening to her. I was able to tell her almost everything I had learned about Lewy Body Dementia with Parkinson's Disease, as well as about the Capgras Syndrome. She listened intently and asked a lot of questions. I told her about her balance issues. I explained as simply as I could the behaviors associated with Capgras Syndrome. She was very worried about becoming a burden to the family and repeated this concern often during our conversation. I'm so glad I got to tell her, when she was in this state of mind, that the family was so good to her because "she was loved very much." I know by her reaction to that she was very grateful and loved the family also.

I told her how difficult it would be for me to place her in a home, and I remember having tears in my eyes. When I mentioned that the kids were helping locate a good home for her, she was very pleased and relieved.

I remember going to bed after this conversation, reflecting on what we were able to convey to each other while Diane appeared to be "in the now" and seemingly understanding what was happening to her. It was one of the most enduring memories I have of our time together while living with Lewy Body Dementia and Parkinson's Disease. These moments are so precious, just knowing we were "together again" for a little while, if ever so briefly.

Sudden realizations

-- Sunday, February 9, 2014 --

I'm back to "another Jim" today. I'm a "kinder" Jim than "the other one." We are also back on the Capgras Syndrome concerning the "other house" and whether all the papers are legal, etc.

I went to Rice Lake after putting a hot dish together. Laurie and Addy stayed with Diane. She had "her Jim" back when I came home. An hour later it was back to the normal "other Jim."

About 9:00 PM, when I was starting to get ready for bed I had an "ah-ha moment!" It suddenly occurred to me that during the 90% of the time I'm the "other Jim," Diane is worse in terms of confusion, Capgras Syndrome, and fear of the "other Jims." She is so much more agitated, constantly questioning me, pacing the floor. It occurred to me that I may be causing Diane's quality of life to be much worse than it should be.

When others are around or when she is talking on the phone one would have a hard time knowing anything was wrong. When Greg or Laurie come over to calm her down, it's always about me, "the other Jim." MY GOD, I may be a real problem for her!

Could it be my focusing on Lewy Body Dementia as a cause for all Diane's actions prevented me from reflecting on my own role in those behaviors? I THINK SO, INDEED. I've forgot to "put myself" in her shoes.

I can only imagine how afraid she must be all the time the "bad Jims" are present. No wonder she is agitated and afraid!

This "aha moment" was totally unexpected. It was the first time I had truly put myself in Diane's shoes. I was so involved in being the best caregiver I could for Diane that I hadn't thought about things from her point of view.

The times Diane was exhibiting fear and abnormal behaviors toward me was when she thought I was an imposter, and this was a majority of the time. Therefore, my constant presence triggered Capgras Syndrome. I reasoned that the visual part of Diane's brain was "seeing" me, but there were no emotional connections made to me as her husband, friend, lover, or father of our children.

My thoughts were moving in several different directions. Would it be better if I were not visible 24 hours a day? Should I just leave the house for a while each day? How often and how long might I have to leave in order for Diane to see me again as "her Jim"? How could I do these things when I was afraid to leave Diane alone?

My constant presence was causing Diane to be living in fear. That made me feel awful.

-- Monday, February 10, 2014 --

I'm a little tired this morning. Diane got up at 1 AM, came to my bedroom, switched the light on and said she didn't know where she was and had to go to the bathroom. She had not turned any lights on to navigate her way down the hall. I got her turned around, but she walked right passed the bathroom door. I showed her the way into the bathroom, but when she was finished she didn't know where the bedroom was. I turned on the hall lights and bedroom lights but needed to walk her to the bed. She was very concerned that I was helping her--we weren't married, and she wondered what people would say. I helped her into bed, shut the lights off, and she went to sleep. I wished I could have fallen asleep.

It's 9:45 AM, and Diane just got up. Today we are in a church setting at the house. The first thing she wanted to know was where Jim was. I told her I didn't know where Jim was. She checked the basement door, but it was dark downstairs. She went back to bed to "rest." As I helped her into bed she wanted to know if the "weekend thing" went OK. I said I've heard no complaints. She said, "Jim says he isn't going to do any more of these things, but he always does."

This comment from Diane rang a bell with me. Since I had retired in 2002, I spent one weekend each month away teaching graduate school for teachers. Her mind must have been retrieving memories of those times. I remember feeling a little guilty about this, as I did tell Diane on several occasions that I would stop teaching sessions that required me to stay in another part of the state for the entire weekend. Diane never complained about my being gone, so I don't know if this was Lewy Body talking or if she had recalled a vivid memory in a morning dream.

Diane told me she fell again this morning but fell into the bed. She also had the dry heaves last night. I didn't hear her, but I did notice the waste basket was next to her bed.

Diane had a very rough time getting to bed tonight. She made a list of her grandchildren and children and when finished she began to cry. She said, "Someone is missing." I checked the list, and everyone was there. I made a list also and showed it to her, but according to Diane there was still someone missing. From listening to her talking and reading I felt she was missing Addy. I emboldened the word Addy on the list and showed it to her. That fixed it!

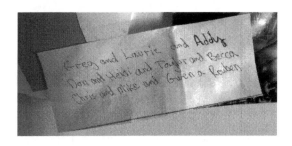

Emphasizing the word "Addy" for Diane

-- Tuesday, February 11, 2014 --

We have an appointment at 3 PM in Rice Lake to invoke the power of attorney for medical care. We left the house at 2 PM so I could drop off a copy of Diane's durable power of attorney at our long-term care insurance company in Barron.

Our appointment turned out to be a meeting between our doctor, her assistant and a social worker. The doctor's assistant took Diane out of the room to do some walking and memory tests. Our doctor asked me a lot of questions about what I observed in Diane's daily activities. She showed me a graph of Diane's weight loss. It was a huge loss in a very short time, a fact we already knew; however, seeing it graphed made it abundantly clear. The doctor asked if I was surprised at the rapid changes in Diane since August, and I said yes, indeed. She encouraged me to find a care center as soon as possible. Her experience with this rapid decline in function was that it will continue at this rapid rate. She recommend that Diane be placed in hospice care as soon as possible. She indicated that six months to live is the usual time frame for care, but some have been in hospice for as long as two years. The truth is if the rapid rate of decline continues it may be only six months.

On the positive side of all this, Diane has said many times she wishes this was over and "the Lord would just take me." I think Diane's prayers are being answered, and it will be sooner rather than a several-year, high-suffering time frame.

This is where the seriousness of Diane's condition became a reality for me. I knew hospice care was recommended for patients with six months to live, but hearing that from the doctor in reference to Diane was a shock. I also knew the doctor had seen countless cases like Diane's. I had confidence in her judgment.

This put a whole different slant on my care-giving and planning for the next several months. I was preparing myself for this disease to take Diane's life in a time span of a few months to two years; however, looking at the data on Diane's weight loss and the rapid progression of the Lewy Body Dementia it was probably going to be more like a few months. I was concerned about Diane's suffering. Her doctor assured me there were several ways to keep Diane as comfortable as possible.

-- Wednesday, February 12, 2014 --

Diane got up at 11:30 PM last night, came into my bedroom and sternly said, "Just what are you doing?"

I said, "Nothing."

She said, "The place is a mess. Dad will be really mad at the mess with the music stuff." (I'm thinking she thought I was one of our children.)

I got up and walked her around the house and into bed again. She went back to sleep. I laid in my bed wondering when she would be at the door again.

Diane got up at 7:30 AM. "Something isn't right," she said. She went into the bathroom and back to bed. This morning, for some reason, she seemed unusually frail. Maybe it's my realization of what the doctor said yesterday.

I went to a Lewy Body Dementia support group in Eau Claire and learned a few new things, mainly the names of books that might be helpful. I didn't learn anything new about the disease or its symptoms, as I've done a lot of Internet research in this area. It was comforting to hear the struggles others are going through and knowing I was not alone.

-- Thursday, February 13, 2014 --

Don, Heidi, and Chris are taking a tour of another memory care center this afternoon.

Don and Heidi called to inform me they found a memory center in Chippewa Falls that might be a great fit for Diane. I got online and looked up the memory care center and agreed. The next day I called the care center to make an appointment for a visit.

A way "outta here" for Diane

-- Friday, February 14, 2014 --

I got up around 6:15 this morning and could see a light in Diane's bedroom. I got dressed and knocked on her door to see if she was OK. She told me she had to urinate so badly she did it in the room. She was afraid to use the bathroom "in the church," so she used the waste basket. I checked and sure enough there was a plastic bag with her sweat pants in it. Everything was soaked in urine. I took the plastic bag out to the garbage, sweat pants and all, then cleaned out the waste basket.

I think this is an example of the type of fear Diane felt most of the time. She was afraid of using the bathroom because she thought it was in a church. She had done her very best not to make a mess in the bedroom by using a plastic bag that was once used to cover a dress. She was ashamed about what had happened, and I felt bad for her. I remember telling her not to worry, accidents happen, and there was no harm done.

I had a Valentine card and a box of candy on the kitchen table this morning. Diane opened the card, stared at it for a while, put it back in the envelope and said nothing. I asked if she wanted a piece of candy after breakfast. She said she already had one. The box hasn't been opened.

I knew after her reaction to the opening and reading of the Valentine card I was not "her Jim" sitting at the table with her. She might have been afraid to say anything because it might have let "this Jim" know she was accepting a gift from him. Given her fears of what people might think of "this Jim" living with her, it makes sense she would not want to show any signs of acceptance.

We are touring a memory care center at 1:30 PM today. Heidi, Chris, and Greg are going with Diane and me. We'll see how this will go.

Diane was happy to see the kids meet us at the center. We walked through the entire facility. Diane thought it was very nice but probably costs too much.

It was comforting to have the kids meet us there. They walked with Diane and asked her questions about what she thought and were enthusiastic about the home. Diane was rather quiet as we walked through the facility. She liked the living room areas with the fireplace and TV and thought the rooms were "cozy" as she put it.

Diane was very concerned with the cost. Even though the insurance or Social Security wouldn't cover the costs in her case, I told her the insurance would cover the costs. This is an explanation I would use many times. I never wanted her to worry about medical costs.

My reaction to visiting the facility was quite different. I wasn't thinking about how nice the place was or all the services they could provide. My thoughts were very conflicted. I had a difficult time visualizing Diane in a memory care center, which was amplified by seeing the condition of some of the residents as we toured. I just wanted to "hang on" to her as long as I could. At the same time, I recalled how Diane's exposure to me 24 hours per day contributed to her fear and anxiety. Even though I knew it was better for Diane, I was having a hard time thinking about her living in a memory care center.

-- Saturday, February 15, 2014 --

I slept in this morning--until almost 7 AM. Diane came in as I was just about to get out of bed. She sat down at the foot of my bed wondering when she could move to the "new place." She is excited to move and is looking things over to see what she should take with her. She said, "It's funny, one day you're moving around OK and the next thing you know you are going to a nursing home." She seems quite aware of what's going on. I checked on her a while ago and she had one clothes basket already packed for the move.

Diane was excited about a "new place" but her statement about going to a nursing home pushed my thoughts again to not wanting her to be there. I had to keep telling myself if I were not around 24 hours per day Diane might be happier. That was reason enough for her to be in a "new place." There is always an emotional trade off coupled with reality while dealing with Lewy Body Dementia.

I notice an increase in Diane's difficulty with swallowing today.

-- Sunday, February 16, 2014 --

Tonight Diane had "her Jim" for a short while. But within a half hour she was seeing me as her boss, a lawyer she once worked for. She was worried about his wife not liking her "staying here."

Diane is in a hurry to move "outta here," as she puts it, to the memory center where she can finally "settle in" some place. She gets angry when it's not tomorrow.

Diane got very angry today about "$28,000 missing from the bank account." That's the first time I've heard ever heard her say "bullshit" as I was trying to explain that the funds weren't missing. It was an error in transferring money from one account to another.

The shock of hearing Diane use such vulgar language delayed my response to her anger. The transferring of money was the only thing I could think of at that instant that might satisfactorily explain what happened. The money transfer story worked, and within a matter of minutes she was no longer concerned. Situations like this often required quick "thinking on my feet" responses.

-- Monday, February 17, 2014 --

The representative from hospice came by. We started the process for getting Diane on hospice care. They work with the memory care center, and a nurse will be visiting us in the near future.

-- Tuesday, February 18, 2014 --

It's a beautiful, clear morning with fresh snow on the ground. Today Louise is coming over to stay with Diane while I make a trip to the

Office of Aging to talk with a benefit specialist. I made a list of questions:

Are there any benefits for the 90 days prior to Diane's long-term care starting? Answer: No.

Is there a difference in benefits for a memory care facility and hospital facilities? Answer: No (they were wrong here as there is a difference).

What if Diane needs hospice for more than six months?
Answer: We can renew it again and again.

What happens to Social Security after the death of a spouse? How do I notify them of her death? Answer: Contact Social Security with a death certificate. Benefits stop the month of death.

At 2 PM Bonnie, a registered nurse, from hospice services came for a visit. She thoroughly explained the hospice services/processes. I signed several forms. She took Diane's temperature, blood pressure, weight, checked lungs and breathing, asked about bowel movements, measured the distance around her arm, and checked out her feet and ankles. Diane weighed 128 pounds in her clothes!

I can't help but notice just how frail Diane is at this point. She is alert but moves very slowly. Her memory and Lewy Body symptoms are about the same. I was "her Jim" a couple of times yesterday. I wonder who I am when someone like the nurse is here.

I called Jack today. He and Connie were shocked to learn Diane is on hospice care--I guess we ALL are!

I'm feeling grief at times, gratitude at times, concern at times, anxiety at times, but most of all I miss my Diane.

Missing Diane seems strange--she was with me all the time. Deep loneliness is perhaps the best way to describe my feelings. I was lonely for the Diane with whom I shared life, conversed, went places, shared thoughts and feelings, and had fun. I had Diane in my presence but only in a physical sense. "My Diane" had left me months ago; yet, I didn't want Diane to move because she was such an integral part of me.

-- Wednesday, February 19, 2014 --

Carrie, the hospice case worker, stopped by to see if we needed anything. She will contact the memory care center to let them know hospice will be working with us.

The care center called this afternoon to let us know that Diane could be admitted if we choose to use their services. The cost for base care is $4,400 per month, and Diane's extra care is $1,290 per month for a total of $5,690 per month. I have some paperwork to complete, but we are ready to move in. They need a couple of days to get everything ready.

Diane needs a TB test before entering the facility.

I called the kids to let them know about the care center.

-- Thursday, February 20, 2014 --

As I was getting my clothes on, I heard Diane come down the hall and ask who was there. She was dressed up in her best clothes. I told her she looked wonderful this morning and asked where she was going. She was dressed for "the funeral." She didn't know who the funeral was for. I was able to get her to change clothes and go back to bed. Sometimes she prepares for her own funeral and thinks she will die suddenly or that she will "get a shot" and it will be all over.

Several times when Diane was preparing for her own funeral, she would worry about the order of service, food, music, etc. Most of the time the funeral was held here at the house, which to her, was a funeral home. Other times, she would think a trip to the clinic for a shot would end everything, or I could give her a shot and "it would be over." There is no question in my mind that Diane wanted her encounter with this disease to be as short as possible.

-- Friday, February 21, 2014 --

We had a major snow storm last night. Greg texted me that if I saw a big John Deere tractor in our driveway, it was a friendly tractor. Laurie's cousin Katie and her husband Josh used their tractor to remove the snow from Greg and Laurie's driveway and came down to do the same in our driveway. Diane stood at the picture window and loved watching the tractor. I'm sure it brought back memories of being on the farm as a youngster.

Josh and his John Deere

-- Saturday, February 22, 2014 --

The last couple of days have been relatively good. I was questioning my decision to have Diane admitted to a memory care center, but today things are back to normal for Diane. There was constant paranoia and delusions over a former boss and his attempt to take the house from us. Hallucinations involving "the other house" or "houses" continue.

Diane said she had dreams last night, and I'm wondering if that might be a result of the Rivastigmine patch. When she took the pills a couple of hours before going to bed there were no dreams. Now, using a patch, Rivastigmine is continuously distributed into her body.

130

Diane can't wait to "get outta here." She doesn't want to wait six more days. That's a hard thing for me to take!

I don't think a day went by, after I started preparing the papers for Diane's admission to the memory care center, when she didn't want "outta here." I'm thankful she isn't fighting us over leaving the house, but it is very hard for me to hear those words, even though I know it is Lewy Body Dementia speaking. No matter how hard I tried, I always fought the feeling, "If I were a better caretaker, Diane might not want to leave."

-- Sunday, February 23, 2014 --

Diane fell again today, her sixth fall. She fell on the table by the recliner. This might be the first time her muscles locked up. She said the front part of her hips didn't work right. She was leaning on the table leaf, but I got there in time to help her regain balance.

Diane had mentioned her hips locking up which was another Parkinson's Disease symptom I was expecting. This fall was not due to a reduction in blood pressure; she didn't tell me it was like floating. This was different. When I heard her complain that her hips didn't work right, I knew Parkinson's Disease symptoms might be taking a new toll on Diane's body.

I noticed a marked increase in REM movements while Diane was sleeping in the chair this afternoon. She also woke herself up talking in her sleep.

As time progressed Diane's sleeping patterns changed. As she slept, I could see a lot of eye movement and small shoulder jerks. Facial expressions changed as her hands and arms moved. Sometimes her hands would move like she was trying to grab something or push something away. There were times when her whole body moved and her arms quickly thrust outward. She would sometimes give out a hauntingly loud, crying sound, causing her to wake up wondering what was happening.

-- Monday, February 24, 2014 --

I arrived at the memory center a little before 1:00 PM and spent half an hour with Cindy, the hospice spiritual counselor. She gave me the names of Diane's case workers and nurse.

I spent two hours reading and signing admission papers for Diane. There is more documentation to protect the organization from liability than for care of the patients, a necessity in our society, I guess.

The drive back from the memory care center was very emotional. It's again the grief at physically missing Diane's presence around the house and the concern that she will be okay staying at the new place. I'm just SO thankful for the time we have had together!

-- Friday, February 28, 2014 --

We are making good progress getting things packed for tomorrow. Diane keeps thinking she is going to have surgery or to get a shot that will "speed things up."

Everything is packed in three clothes baskets, a couple of boxes, and placed on the floor ready for tomorrow: moving day.

Diane gets "outta here," the move to memory care

-- Saturday, March 1, 2014 --

It's moving day for Diane, such an emotional roller coaster. I'm sad to think of her not being with me on a daily basis, yet glad for the care she will have at the memory care center. I am happy she will be able to see Don, Chris, Greg, and her siblings more consistently. I'm internally crying in one instant and organizing the move in another, trying to think a few days and weeks ahead, then getting back to "now" before the cycle continues.

Diane on moving day

We moved Diane into the memory care center about 1 PM. Greg and I got the large items moved in. Then, after Mike and Chris came, we moved the baskets and boxes into to Diane's room. Don and Heidi came and the girls put everything in drawers. I'm just not sure Diane understands everything that's going on. Bless her heart for being such a mild-mannered person.

I had a very teary drive home and had a long cry when I got into bed. This is hard!

This was a night of deep grieving. I cried long and hard, literally crying myself to sleep. The past week had been so intense, getting Diane ready for the move, that I had no time to think or reflect. The last time I had some reflection time was the trip home from the memory care center after signing the admission papers, which was also a tearful time. I felt deep concern for Diane, not knowing what she was feeling, and was fearful of her first night in a strange place with strange people surrounding her. There was guilt about putting her in a care center and, at the same time, grief at losing my life-long partner. I felt angry at Lewy Body Dementia with Parkinson's Disease. My mind was running wild with sad and angry emotions.

The following is an introduction used at the memory care center to introduce Diane to the staff along with notes from Diane's first day there.

(All memory care notes are in _New Times Roman Italics_ from this point on.)

My name is Diane, and I am moving to LHMC (Lake Hallie Memory Care) from my home where I live with my husband Jim. I have Lewy Body Dementia and Parkinson's Disease. My dementia has progressed quickly, and I no longer always recognize my husband. At times, I feel he is an intruder, and it causes situations where he needs to leave the room or the house until our son comes over and assures me that Jim truly is my husband.

I also have hallucinations. I see people in the room who are not there. I do not, at this point, become frightened of them, but I will become flustered when all of a sudden I no longer see them.

I will at times think that I am at a church or scout camp and sometimes may see two or three of my husband at the same time and think that he is three different people.

134

This is very hard on all of my family. I have metastatic colon cancer, and due to my dementia, treatment for the cancer would be hard for me to understand or to cooperate in following doctor's orders. I have a colostomy and, up to this point, have been caring for it on my own. But my dementia has caused me to forget at times how to complete the task. I have just been put on the hospice program, and they will be coming to LHMC to see me and to give instructions on my cares.

1:44 PM Resident just arrived here at LHMC. Resident is visiting with family right now and walked around the building. Fifteen minute checks for 72 hours.

9:53 PM Resident refused assistance with PM cares and toileting. Resident's colostomy bag was emptied. Resident visited with family and ate dinner in Bravo side dining room. Resident refused to go to the movie for activities but went to the ballet performance. Resident was seen back in her room after dinner and stayed there. Fifteen minute checks were complete and vitals were taken. Resident was very confused wondering where her husband was, stating she would wait for him to come pick her up. No concerns.

I only read these notes in the process of writing the book. Knowing that Diane was wondering where I was and waiting for me to pick her up brought back bouts with grief. I think reading these on a daily basis would have been a detriment to my interaction with Diane during my visits while she was at the center.

-- Sunday, March 2, 2014 --

I got a message from Greg that Diane had called him at midnight. I called her about 8:30 AM to see if she needed help. The problem was she was worried about me! Wow!

When I got to the memory care center, Diane was sitting in her chair and got up to give me a big hug. I noticed that she had taken everything out of the drawers and filled the clothes basket in the bathroom. Other things were put in the toy crate that we brought for Gwenyth and Reuben when they visit Diane. Her clothes were all

removed from the closet and laid on top of the basket. She thought she was moving again.

It was wonderful to get that hug from Diane. Being "her Jim" filled my heart with joy. Her packing everything up and putting the items in the clothes basket didn't matter. I was her husband, her Jim again.

We'll have to get Diane a landline as she can't use the cell phone. She can't use the number buttons or get the order of numbers right. I tried calling many times tonight and got voice mail. Pushing buttons won't work. She needs to simply pick up the receiver and answer.

6:44 AM Resident was up and assisted with getting ready for the day. Resident came out into the living room and visited with this staff and another resident for a while and then walked the halls a little. Then she stated she wanted to lay down until breakfast.

10:27 AM Resident refused any assistance from staff with cares and was independent with toileting needs. Resident is currently with a visitor who came this AM.

8:51 PM Resident has been in her room throughout the afternoon. Resident didn't eat much for dinner, about 10%, and went back to her room. Resident kept looking for her husband and asking for two little girls. This writer told resident that her husband is not here and no little girls around.

-- Monday, March 3, 2014 --

I arrived at Diane's room about 9:30 AM. All her clothes were again packed away in the clothes basket ready for another move.

We went on a couple of walks around the facility, and Diane did well. We had good conversation, but there was still much paranoia over a former boss and our house papers.

Not having me around 24 hours a day seemed to be reduce the Capgras Syndrome. I was still her Jim. Of course, I had no way of knowing what was happening in Diane's mind while she was without me at the memory center. It was a relief to have her recognize me as her husband. We were able to talk, and I was able to put myself in her mind well enough to carry out a conversation. Her paranoia over the house papers and former boss was still present. Not having access to the satisfaction of deed made it a little more difficult to convince her that things were in good order.

2:00 AM Resident stayed in bed for breakfast, ate half a piece of toast, and stayed in room for most of the morning. A visitor came at 9:45 and stayed till lunch time. Resident said she and her husband ate out this afternoon. Not sure if this is true, due to them not leaving the building.

-- Tuesday, March 4, 2014 --

I took Diane's long term care insurance application to Rice Lake for her doctor to complete.

I got down to see Diane about 1:30 PM. She was glad to see me and wondered what had happened to me. There are many times when she thinks the memory care center is a church, wondering what time services are.

I moved all my clothes back into our bedroom tonight and slept in my own bed for the first time since November.

I felt like our bedroom belonged to Diane. Moving all my clothes back seemed awkward. Even without Diane in the house, I was checking in the bedroom to see if the light was on or off. It had been the normal "first thing to do" in the morning when I got up.

-- Wednesday, March 5, 2014 --

Diane had a busy day. I got there a little after 2 PM. Our friend Mary came around 2:30 PM, Chris and the kids came a little later, and then Mary's son and family also visited. Little Gwenyth loves to dance to the music in the activity room, and the residence just love to see her and little Reuben dance and play.

-- Thursday, March 6, 2014 --

Today at 2:30 PM I will meet the Chippewa Falls hospice nurse in Diane's room.

7:00 AM Resident slept in and said that she felt so much better this morning. Also resident requested to have breakfast and then a shower. Resident ate 100 % of breakfast and thoroughly enjoyed her shower. Resident was about to attend activities when a family member came to visit. Resident was taken to activities after lunch and is still in the bistro making new friends and enjoying the olympics.

8:46 PM Resident refused to put on pajamas tonight stating that she was more comfortable in her clothes. This writer tried three times to change her mind, and she still felt more comfortable in her clothes. Resident ate well for supper then sat in her room and read the newspaper. Resident is now in bed with eyes closed.

-- Sunday, March 9, 2014 --

I spent the morning with Diane. While we were sitting and chatting the landline phone buzzed, and I could hear a dial tone. A phone technician came in to check if the phone worked. It did.

I called Diane a little before 7 PM. She said she wasn't doing well. There were some bad kids trying to give the grandkids drinks, and she was afraid. I told her where each of the kids were and assured her they were all OK. She was also having trouble lowering the blinds on her window. I asked her to get help from the caregiver at the desk outside her room. She said she would do that.

I was very pleased that Diane was able to call me on the new landline phone. I set it up to dial by pressing a single key, which only dialed me. That way others would not get midnight or early morning calls. It was always painful to hear Diane say she wasn't doing well. It often took several minutes of explanation before she could be convinced that things were okay. I think she related to my voice quite well. The phone required only audio communications, so the lack of correlation between audio and visual brain passages causing Capgras Syndrome was stifled. This was a small victory over Capgras Syndrome.

-- Monday, March 10, 2014 --

Greg and I went to Rice Lake at 6 PM to see a bluegrass concert. My banjo teacher's band opened for the show. It was a great evening, the first time I've been at an event since August 2013. It was good to get out.

7:30 PM Resident became very confused and weepy, saying things were moved in her room and people were destroying evidence, that she couldn't have her shampoo or TV remote in her room because the DNA would be destroyed. She walked around the facility for a while, then stated that she would go to her room, but she would not lay down. Resident is now in her room with light on looking through some papers.

-- Tuesday, March 11, 2014 --

We met with the hospice nurse, Courtney, at 9 AM. Diane said she didn't sleep well last night. She said she had problems with staff members and was not nice to them. We believe she was dreaming, but it was very real to Diane. She was upset about homosexuals she saw in a room as she passed by. She didn't want to talk about it, but Courtney and I convinced her to share her thoughts as long as nobody else was listening. It was hard to understand how the brain can conjure up such thoughts. In general, Diane seemed more incoherent. Hallucinations and perceptions are getting worse. While looking out her window at the road and weeds she said there were snowmobilers on the roof.

We couldn't find the TV remote, as Diane had put in under some clothes in the closet. She was able to turn the TV on and off. But even this is difficult.

The care center called late in the afternoon. Diane was very confused and wanted to talk to me. We talked for a while, and she wanted to go home. She was crying. After the call, so was I.

The "wanting to go home" calls were emotional for Diane, as well as me. I tried to put myself in Diane's mind during these calls by imagining her as a young child left for the first time at a friend's house and becoming homesick. Most of the time, I was able to convince her to remain where she was until morning, and then I or someone else would pick her up and take her home. Diane wanted to go home but didn't know where home was--it was just "home," and home was where her mind wanted to be. I wondered if home was the home farm, our house in Chetek, one of the houses on the hill she often referred to, or maybe it was her heavenly home. Whatever "home" was, I couldn't take her there.

9:29 PM Resident spent most of the PM shift wandering the halls and visiting with staff. Resident was very confused today and having hallucinations. Staff just kept redirecting her and comforting her. Staff also had her call her husband to talk to him, and he thanked us for that! Resident is currently in her room with no other concerns at this time.

9:37 PM Hospice Order: Resident has been having hallucinations and told hospice RN that she is unsure of who to trust or who she can talk to during those times. Hospice RN indicated that resident at times realizes that what she is seeing is not real but still feels unsure of who to tell about it. Hospice RN and husband have asked coordinator to go in and speak to resident for about 1/2 hour each day for the next week so that resident begins to feel comfortable confiding in her. Husband indicated that resident's hallucinations have decreased since moving to LHMC, and he is very glad to see this.

-- Thursday, March 13, 2014 --

I left to visit Diane about 12:30 PM and arrived at 5 PM. Diane had once again packed everything up to move again. Everything was unplugged, the TV antenna was even disconnected. I just put everything back while we were visiting.

Connecting electronic devices was something Diane always wanted me to do. It was difficult to unplug the TV from the wall outlet because it was behind the clothes closet. I had a hard time plugging it in when I set it up. I think Diane was pretty determined to disconnect everything before "moving."

Diane is still very reluctant to get involved with activities. She also has a difficult time knowing where she is and what day/time it is.

It's been very difficult to see Diane in this environment, yet I really don't know what I would do if she were at home.

9:50 AM When staff went to get resident for breakfast, she stated, "What is going on now, the reception for the wedding?" Staff stated, "There is no wedding reception today. It's time for breakfast." Resident stated, "Okay." Resident's feet are swollen, and she had a hard time putting her shoes on. Staff found a pair of shoes that stretched and zipped. They were a little tight but resident stated that they felt just fine.

8:21 PM Resident has been walking around the quad confused and looking for brothers and sisters and mom and dad. Resident is pleasant when redirecting.

-- Friday, March 14, 2014 --

When I walked into Diane's room, she was in the bathroom. I waited for a while. When she didn't come out I knocked on the door and asked how she was doing. She opened the door and said she had a mess. There was stool from her ostomy pouch all over her, on her clothes, and on the floor. I put on a pair of the plastic gloves and cleaned her up, put her clothes in a plastic bag, and cleaned the floor and her shoes. I don't know what happened.

Don came to visit. Diane was crying and confused while Don was there. He came over to her and held her hand. Both had tears in their eyes. So did I. It was so heartening to see Don do this. It was a magic moment in my life!

Don, our oldest son, had a difficult time seeing his mother in the condition she was in. That afternoon, when Diane was having a bad time and crying, it was difficult for both Don and me. Don moved to her and held her hand, just as she had done so many times when he was a child and needed comforting. It was a role reversal that affected me deeply. Diane leaned her head on Don's shoulders, and it didn't take long for her to feel better. What a wonderful thing for a dad to see.

141

9:16 PM Resident was hallucinating tonight and was seeing little children in her room. Resident asked writer to remove the kids.

-- Saturday, March 15, 2014 --

I spent the afternoon with Diane. She is still very confused about where she is, paranoid over locked doors, and thinks the food is the same all the time. She has problems finding her room when we go for a walk around the building square.

It's been two weeks today that Diane moved into the memory care center. Every day I've left the center I have had tears in my eyes which continue as I drive home. It's difficult to see Diane in the condition she is in. But I'm grateful for the wonderful life we had together before Lewy Body/Parkinson's took over.

-- Sunday, March 16, 2014 --

Today I went to our church for the first time in months. It was good to be there but quite emotional as Diane wasn't sitting with me.

I was planning to stay home all day today, but I just couldn't. I had to get down to see Diane for a little while. I got to the memory center a little before 3:00 PM. Diane was in her room. She had been doing most of the activities but left during Bingo because a couple of the men were too loud for her. She absolutely couldn't understand that she was at the memory care center in Chippewa Falls and I was staying in Chetek.

I don't know how to explain the feeling of needing to be with Diane as much as possible; yet, I was afraid if I spent too much time with her, the Capgras Syndrome would return along with the "other Jims." I had been "her Jim" since she moved into the memory care center. When I was "her Jim," we could converse, particularly when talking about our children and grandchildren.

6:23 AM Resident was up, told staff she had to go--it was 3:30 AM. She was told that it was 3:30 AM and too early to be going anywhere. She

142

said, "Oh my gosh. OK, I'll go back to bed, thank you." She has been in bed since, and her eyes are closed.

-- Monday, March 17, 2014 --

Greg and I arrived at the memory center around 9:30 AM. Diane was sitting in her chair. When I asked how she was doing, she said, "Waiting for you." She didn't take a shower because the door to the hall was open a crack. She was in good spirits but still can't figure out where she is and where I am staying.

Mel called tonight. He had been to visit Diane this afternoon. He said they had a good visit but often Diane wouldn't make sense when talking.

Diane's brother Mel

8:52 AM Resident is out of Rivastigmine and it was ordered. I contacted pharmacy as the patch had not arrived. I was informed they are awaiting insurance. I also contacted hospice to see if there is anything they could do to speed up the process. Hospice nurse will be in today to see resident. Pharmacy delivered at 2:30 PM. I also faxed the doctor. Management is aware and will take care of the issue.

Health insurance company interference happened way too often. This is one of the failures of our healthcare system. These companies are nothing more than money launderers between patients, their doctors, clinics, and hospitals. They contribute nothing to the direct care of the patients. I became angry each time they delayed medication or refused coverage. My feeling was, and is, that insurance companies have no right to delay any medicines, refuse a doctor's treatment, or refuse to cover a prescribed medicine. A system that makes profits from people's illness is morally wrong.

-- Wednesday, March 19, 2014 --

Diane called a little before 4:00 PM today. She said she needed money to pay a "ticket." It seems she broke a small dish in her room and thought she would be fined for it.

1:32 PM Resident was dressed when this writer came in and was told by staff she "was good to go." Later saw resident did not have a colostomy bag on and she had a bit of a mess on her underwear. Area was cleaned and applied new colostomy bag.

-- Thursday, March 20, 2014 --

Last night is the first night that I can remember since Diane moved to the memory center that I didn't get teary-eyed before going to sleep.

I visited Diane about 9:30 AM. She had just finished her breakfast and still didn't have any water. I straightened up the room, made the bed, and hung up some of her clothes. It's hard to know what clothes are in need of washing, as she keeps taking the clothes out and transferring them from one place to another. The TV was unplugged again.

9:07 PM Resident was having issues --someone getting murdered and her having to call 911. She tried using the phone to call. Staff reassured her and said that there was no murder and that everything was okay. Resident is now in room.

Gwenyth left, Addy right

-- Friday, March 21, 2014 --

Today I'll have Addy with me all day. She had not visited the memory center and thought it was a nice place for Grandma to be.

Mel visited Diane in the afternoon and called me around 5:00 PM. He spent about 45 minutes with her. He said it was harder to have a conversation today and that she was paranoid over her purse--a very normal thing.

Chris, Mike, Addy, Gwen, and Reuben with Diane at the care center

9:48 PM Resident did not want to get ready for bed tonight. Staff found her in the bathroom today with BM all over and her colostomy bag missing. She said she threw it away but staff could not find it. Staff gave her a new bag. She was pretty worried tonight about where her family was and when she was leaving. She walked the halls most of the night.

-- Saturday, March 22, 2014 --

I arrived at Diane's about 9:45 AM. She was wandering about the halls and talking with a couple of the staff members. She was carrying her purse and waiting for me to come. I found her very confused. We sat down in the dining area where it was quiet, a good place to talk. Some things that came out were my testifying at a hearing, guys cutting triangle openings in her room/door, ladies with good voices upstairs, selling our house up north, a funeral in the room so we have to move, etc. She seems to be getting quite unsteady as she walks, at least more than I've observed in the last few weeks.

This was the first time I could not relate to anything Diane was talking about. It was impossible to have a conversation. She seemed to know me as her husband, but her thoughts seemed to be random. There were things that were thematic, such as a funeral in the room or selling the house up north. But my testifying at a hearing must have been from some of Diane's memories of working at a lawyer's office (I have never testified in a courtroom). Voices from upstairs might be memories of many musical performances we had attended. When we walked to her room she held on tightly to my arm and didn't let go until she sat in her chair.

The random thoughts and noticeable unsteadiness when she walked made this a rough day.

9:34 AM Resident refused to change her clothes or have assistance with her cares. She was crying and asking if her husband was still singing. She walked the halls around the facility. After breakfast she did allow staff to assist her with her colostomy bag. She is still waiting for her family to come. When asked how she is, she will reply, "Terrible." Resident's husband came to visit after breakfast, which seemed to help. She is attending afternoon activities.

9:01 PM Resident seemed to be hallucinating during PM cares as she kept waving and carrying on a conversation with no one. No other concerns.

-- Sunday, March 23, 2014 --

I visited Diane about 9:30 AM. She was watching the church services on the TV in the large room. Her memory, in terms of conversation, is getting more disjointed as time goes on. She is very "in tune" to hearing conversations outside her door. Even the wall TV in the next room seems to trigger random thoughts.

10:12 PM Resident was assisted with some cares. Resident would not let this writer do some of the cares. When asked why she didn't want some help, resident stated that she is leaving with her car as soon as it gets out of the shop. Resident was very agitated tonight and confused. Resident is sitting in her room now waiting to leave in her car.

-- Monday, March 24, 2014 --

I got to Diane's about 9:30 AM. She was doing exercises as I peeked in. The activity facilitator, Helen, motioned me to step back. I did.

Helen caught me in the hall and said Diane has had a tough morning. Helen brought her back to the room, and Diane and I visited until just before lunch. I don't recall any parts of our conversation making any kind of sense or logic. Diane was talking about wedding ceremonies where everyone was re-taking their vows. She did recall when she and I did that in Colorado, but this wasn't the same. She is still concerned about our second house--did it sell? Did it have a certain number of acres? Who was interested? This is a recurring theme.

-- Tuesday, March 25, 2014 --

We met with the hospice nurse today. Diane's vitals look good. The insurance company has decided that they will no longer pay for the Rivastigmine used to help with hallucinations. This happened a week ago, and the people at the memory center got hold of our doctor's office for an OK. It really makes me angry that insurance companies can make these decisions over a doctor's authority. I wish they were out of the health care loop.

11:02 PM Resident was very restless and anxious tonight. She walked the halls for most of the night and would not let staff help her or show her directions. She made comments about getting out of here and about getting out of jail. She told another resident to get away from here when walking in the hall. She set off the door alarms too.

As I visited Diane, many residents wandered about. Some would try to get out the doors causing alarms to go off. I remember thinking, "I hope Diane won't be doing the same thing." She wanted continually to "get outta of here" when she was at home, but she never tried to leave without me being with her. At the memory care center I noticed a significant change. She took things to another level by trying to open the doors to get out.

-- Wednesday, March 26, 2014 --

I felt mentally drained when I got home. Diane called. I was pleased she got the phone to work. I spent half an hour this morning trying to teach her to pick up the phone and press the small green "A" button.

I had a strange feeling last night after dinner. It was a deep "in the stomach" feeling, like wanting to cry but not being able to--like a distant loneliness--realizing I'm without Diane here forever, or like forgetting something very important. It's likely part of the grieving process.

This feeling came often on my drives home after leaving Diane, but this was the first experience at home. It suddenly came on while I was sitting in the living room relaxing. It was a very uncomfortable feeling, similar to the feeling I had after taking down the Christmas tree and realizing I had lost Diane to Lewy Body Dementia and Parkinson's Disease on December 13, 2013. The best way I can describe the feeling is like suddenly realizing you have lost something of great value that can't be replaced.

-- Thursday, March 27, 2014 --

I picked up Diane's ostomy pouches at the drugstore this morning only to find that they were $50 more than I usually pay because the insurance company didn't recognize the claim. Another insurance battle! I just hold my breath any time I open an envelope from the health insurance company fearing a huge bill for something "not covered." I'm disliking the health/insurance bookkeeping nightmare more all the time.

The nurse at the memory center informed me that they put Diane back on Rivastigmine because she was much more confused last week. UGH!

-- Friday, March 28, 2014 --

I arrived at the memory care center a little before 9:00 AM. Diane had just gotten up and was sitting in her chair. A staff member was taking her vitals. She said Diane was a little shaky this morning. Diane was shivering even though she said she wasn't cold. It was more like tremors. She began telling me about an incident last night. Don and Heidi were sleeping in her bed and she was in her chair trying to sleep. She couldn't get the words out because of the tremors/shivering. I have not seen anything like this before.

Courtney, the hospice nurse, came about 20 minutes into this incident. Diane told us everyone was waiting for me, the last to come, before it happened. It was her, Diane, dying and everyone was there. She said Don was very calm considering the situation. She said it was very real. She told us the vision/dream made her quite anxious.

After sharing this Diane ate a piece of toast with coffee and seemed to lose the tremors/shivering.

Also, hospice will cover the cost of the Rivastigmine patches. I need to find out why our insurance wouldn't pay for the patches.

I was very concerned for Diane as I sat there listening to her tell about her "dream." Her mouth would quiver as she tried to tell us about what she saw. It was such a violent quiver that it made her sound as if she were stuttering. Her whole body shook as she talked. I thought all the possible tremors associated with Parkinson's Disease were manifesting themselves all at once. When Diane revealed that it was her death, and I was the one everyone was waiting for, I hurt inside. I felt like she was telling me her death was going to happen soon and she wanted me there. It was an emotional, uncomfortable feeling.

-- Saturday, March 29, 2014 --

I found Diane a little tired this morning. She had another "dream" last night. She started telling me about the mess she made last night in the car when she couldn't get to the bathroom in time. It all involved a concert at the Cameron bluegrass place. Mel and Bill were playing, Bill on banjo and Mel on guitar. I asked if it sounded good, and she said, "Pretty good." Words and thoughts are very mixed up. Hopefully having the Rivastigmine back will help. At least we now will have a baseline of sorts since she was off it for a week or so. I'm also wondering if the other Jims might be coming back. We were in the hall walking, and she saw the person that she thought was Roger, her brother. When I explained that her brother Roger lived in Galesville, WI, she asked, rather abruptly, how I knew that. That's what she would do when the other Jims were active--spying to know things about her family.

1:43 PM Resident stated to staff, "I feel so embarrassed because I couldn't find my way to the bathroom during the night. I just couldn't hold it anymore, so I wet myself." Staff reassured her and told her it will be okay. So staff changed her bedding and washed her clothes. Staff was notified and suggested that maybe when she goes to bed that staff should turn her light on in her bathroom and that maybe she should wear a pad or something at night. Resident ate in her room for breakfast due to the accident this morning.

-- Sunday, March 30, 2014 --

I arrived at the memory center at 9:30 AM and found Diane sitting in her chair dozing. She is continually confused about the center being a church, her room being a house, my living in Chetek, and how long she has been at the center. She thought I was working with the Amish on a farm and worried I was working too hard. I think she saw or recalls the movie Witness. As we were walking down the hall she said, "I hope this doesn't take long." She meant it didn't take long to pass away. Breaks my heart!

Even though Diane and I had many conversations about death and dying, death is a difficult reality for the mind to grasp. Diane expressed to me again that she didn't want to linger on in the state she was in. She said it in such a matter-of-fact way. I remember replying, "I hope so too." As soon as I said that, I wanted to take it back. I didn't want her to think I wanted her to die soon. She didn't say anything more, we just continued our walk down the hallway. I think Diane knew what I was saying.

A second month at memory care

-- Thursday, April 3, 2014 --

6:00 PM Resident joined every activity in the bistro: exercises, church service, and ping-pong toss. Resident ate well with others and walked the halls for exercise. Resident seemed to be in a good mood today and is smiling and socializing with staff often.

10:30 PM Resident was out with husband until 5:45 PM. She attended music this evening and spent the rest of the night in her room.

-- Friday, April 4, 2014 --

Diane called twice this afternoon. It was good that she was able to dial me. We had a nice chat. Courtney the hospice nurse called to say she visited Diane and she taught one of the staff members to change Diane's pouch. Courtney also asked about what seemed to her as swelling beneath Diane's stoma area. I had also noticed it but thought it was normal with the considerable weight loss. Courtney is going to check with our doctor

Diane called a couple of times today, and we had good phone conversations. She was worried about how to get both cars "down there." She also was also able to get her TV turned on with my directions over the phone.

1:05 PM Some distention around the area of the stoma. It is firm to the touch, resident denied pain. Hospice on site and is researching this.

10:56 PM Writer checked colostomy bag and it was empty. Resident had mechanical soft food for dinner. Resident was assisted with PM cares and is now in bed with eyes closed. Resident was very pleasant all shift.

-- Saturday, April 5, 2014 --

9:36 PM Resident walked the halls and socialized with other residents. Resident also enjoyed popcorn and soda in the bravo living room while watching a movie with other residents. Resident believes she is going on a trip tomorrow and has packed some of her clothing in a pillow case. Resident is now in bed with eyes closed.

-- Sunday, April 6, 2014 --

10:43 AM Resident appeared confused and agitated as she was asking what time the bus was coming to get her. This writer told her it was Sunday and the bus would not be coming today. Resident then asked if her husband was picking her up and was told he should be here to see her by 10:00 AM. Resident was crying and said she was so confused and writer reassured her it was going to be OK. Resident's husband came to visit at 9:30 AM, and by this time resident appeared calmer and happier. This writer went into resident's room to see if they needed anything and resident apologized for acting horribly this morning. Writer reassured her she did not act horribly and was happy to help, and this made her smile. No other concerns at this time.

-- Monday, April 7, 2014 --

I visited Diane about 9:50 AM this morning. She had just been visited by Courtney, our hospice nurse. Diane had a sad morning as she was realizing that she was in a "hospital" environment and didn't understand why she was there. She was rather quiet during my visit. As I was taking her down the hall to noon lunch, she began to sob and tear up. So did I. We both went back to the room, hugged each other and sat down to talk. After a minute or so she changed completely, wanting to get to lunch and worried about her hair looking OK. We went to the lunchroom and Diane went right in and sat by Barbara, the lady we played Bingo with a week ago. It was hard for me to leave her today, and I had more tears on the drive home.

10:19 PM Resident is refusing to go to bed at this time and wants cares done when she is ready to sleep.

-- Tuesday, April 8, 2014 --

I got to the memory care center at 9:30 AM. Diane was in her exercise activity. She was smiling and laughing with all the participants. When she saw me I went over and sat behind her until they were finished, then we walked back to her room. I asked how she was doing and she said she was worried that I'd been in an accident last night and nobody would give her any information.

12:49 PM Resident was very confused and having hallucinations of people coming into her room stealing her stuff. She was pretending to shoot them. I did my best to assure her she is safe and her things are safe as well. She asked for her husband. I said he would be in later. She just kept repeating, "Oh, something doesn't seem right!" Her husband did stop for a visit this morning.

-- Wednesday, April 9, 2014 --

I arrived at the memory center at 9:40 AM to find Diane in the hallway meeting me and asking me what I was smiling about--she had teary eyes. She was upset about missing Chris and Mike's wedding and party last night. She was upset because no one could tell her anything about it. We went in her room and sat on the bed. I explained that she didn't miss any wedding party last night, and that Chris and Mike were married several years ago and have two children. She asked if the sickness she has made her imagine the wedding. I explained that her illness will cause this to happen. She began to feel a little better. We played a few rounds of Solitaire until she felt tired and wanted to sleep a while. I left about 11:00 AM, just as Helen, the activities director, brought her little dog to see Diane. Diane loved the little dog and enjoyed petting her.

Each time I traveled to the memory center, about a 45-minute drive from our house, I wondered what Diane would be like when I got there. I never knew what to expect. I always approached her with a positive outlook and a smile. Most of the time she was glad to see me and would give me a hug.

154

This day was different. Diane was not happy to see me, she didn't want a hug, and was very upset with me about not keeping her informed of Chris and Mike's wedding party. Needless to say, I lost my cheery greeting and smile.

Now and then Diane would ask me if her illness made her imagine things like a wedding. I always felt when she asked a question like that she was in a state that would allow me to talk logically with her. It seemed like it was a time when Diane could self reflect.

-- Friday, April 11, 2014 --

10:56 AM Resident ate 80% for both breakfast and lunch, but refused all morning activities. Resident has been staying in her room and is very depressed. Hospice is here and has been notified.

2:40 PM Courtney, hospice, wrote an order to have resident on 15-minute checks through the weekend to provide support to the resident. Hospice would like staff to be visiting with resident on each check to let her know that there is always someone around for her to visit with throughout the day. Resident was introduced to resident from A 106, and they have been visiting throughout the day today. Fifteen minute checks have been implemented through Sunday night.

10:52 PM Resident had a great evening, singing along with others in the bistro, and having fun with her newfound friend. Her son also came to visit and they took walks outside. At dinnertime, writer sat with resident to eat her meal and husband came and was happy to see that she was in a good mood and not alone. Resident was very active today and went to sleep early.

-- Sunday, April 13, 2014 --

Today is Palm Sunday. Diane did very well today. She held little Reuben while he drank from his bottle. She enjoyed the company and chatting with everyone. She was quite tired around 4:00 PM and wanted to go home, thinking it was home in Chetek or Northfield, I'm not sure which. She was worried that the apartment where she is staying was going to be closed.

155

Diane with Reuben

-- Monday, April 14, 2014 --

Diane called at 5:00 AM this morning. She was wondering when I was coming home and told me that I should pick her up at the church. I told her I would pick her up there at 9:00 AM, and we would be meeting with Courtney the hospice nurse.

We met with Courtney and decided to reduce the number of pills Diane takes each day by not taking some of the vitamins. We are going to try changing the meds used for her depression. She is maxed out on Sertraline. Hopefully this will help with some of the sadness and watery eyes Diane is having during the times I'm not there or others are visiting.

Diane called while I was meeting at Barron County Campus. She needed the car keys but thought she was calling Greg. We got it straightened out by letting her know that I had the car.

10:00 PM Resident was checked every 25 minutes throughout the PM shift and assisted as needed. Resident did not attend dinner or 6 PM activity. When getting resident up to do PM cares, resident was very unsteady with walking and could not keep her eyes open. This staff member and another staff had to assist the resident to the bathroom.

10:35 PM Resident was given a new medication tonight: Mirtazapine. When doing PM cares she was very drowsy and had a very hard time walking. It took two people to walk her to the bathroom and to bed. Drowsiness is a side effect, but for the night put her on Fifteen minute checks for safety reasons.

-- Tuesday, April 15, 2014 --

About 10:15 AM, friends Alyce and Pat came to visit. It was a wonderful visit. We had some good conversation and visited until Diane was called to dinner. I walked Alyce and Pat to their car. I explained what Lewy Body Dementia with Parkinson's was and why Diane had been placed in hospice care. They were very surprised about how fast the disease was progressing. (They aren't the only ones!)

Diane called tonight around 5:45 PM. She was wondering if she had to get things ready to move. We had a good half-hour chat about why she was there, why I was in Chetek, and why we couldn't stay together. These are very hard conversations. I miss her deeply.

9:39 PM Resident refused to attend activities.

10:29 PM Resident is currently walking around her room. When asked what she is doing, resident stated, "I am looking for matches." Writer asked why, and resident stated, "For the guys who are trying to shoot us." Writer explained that no one was around when writer came in, so they must have left. Resident stated, "That is good." Resident continues to walk around her room and occasionally peek out of her room. Writer will continue to monitor resident.

-- Wednesday, April 16, 2014 --

I got a call from Diane around 5:45 PM. She was so upset she couldn't get her words out and trembled as she talked. I talked with a staff member who asked if I could come down to help get Diane settled down. I left at 6:05 PM.

Diane had gone to dinner and sat down to eat. The staff member went to get another resident. When she returned Diane was gone. They did a building search but initially couldn't find her. They found Diane hiding behind her chair crouched down on her knees and very upset. She was packing things to leave. There was a wedding she was missing, and she was very confused. Knowing how to comfort Diane during times like this is often difficult.

6:10 PM Resident was taken to the dining room for dinner this evening. Staff left the area to bring more residents in; when staff returned to the dining room the resident was no longer there. Staff began looking for resident. She was found hiding in the corner of her bedroom behind a rocking chair. Resident was on her knees shaking. When staff asked resident what was wrong she stated, "I can't move or he is going to shoot my family." Staff asked who was going to shoot her family, and she stated, "The man standing behind me." This writer reassured resident that she would be safe here and that all staff members are here to protect her. After several minutes of reassuring resident of her safety she was able to stand up with staff.

Resident struggled to both stand and walk, possibly due to sitting on her knees for an unknown period of time. Resident was redirected to sit at the edge of her bed. Staff encouraged resident to join her housemates for dinner. She continually stated, "Just go on to the party without me. I'm not going down there, everyone will just point and laugh at me like they always do." Staff again reassured resident this would be untrue and that they would enjoy the resident's company at dinner. She then began talking about the man that was going to kill her and her family but struggled to do so and began stumbling for words. She began shaking excessively.

Resident's husband was called. She began crying more intensely and breathing more quickly. Staff talked to husband on the phone, updating him on tonight's incident. Hospice was notified as well. They advised staff to ask husband to come in to see resident. Hospice will notify Courtney of incident, and she will then contact the MD. Husband was contacted and is currently on his way.

When Diane called she sounded like she did when she was trying to tell the hospice nurse and me about seeing bad people in the memory center. She couldn't get the words out and sounded like someone with severe stuttering. I wished there were some kind of *Star Trek* transporter that would have beamed me instantly to Diane. The waiting and not knowing what to expect on my way to the center kept my mind overly active with questions like, "Was it the drugs? Did the Lewy Body Dementia take a sudden and horrible turn? What would trigger such an incident? Could Diane hurt herself?"

When I got to the center the staff gave me a briefing on what had occurred. I comforted Diane by putting my arms around her, speaking softly, and just holding her tightly. Internally I was feeling deep sorrow for her. After what seemed like several minutes she became a little more relaxed. The crying and stuttering had diminished prior to my arrival. I could talk to her, and she would answer. I could tell she was emotionally drained. She had not eaten dinner, having refused to go to the dining area. It was a very emotional evening.

I was thankful for the staff at the memory center and their handling of the situation. They were kind, considerate, and highly respectful of Diane and her condition. I was very appreciative of their calling me to come down to be with Diane. I had gotten to know several of the staff during the couple months Diane was there, and they had always given me a short brief when I arrived each day about how Diane had done during the afternoon and evening when I wasn't there. I remember feeling a sense of relief as I drove home (again, teary-eyed) that we had found an excellent memory care center for Diane.

-- Thursday, April 17, 2014 --

I arrived at the memory center a little before 10:00 AM. Diane was in the activities room and doing pretty well with the others. I put things away in her room (she was packed for a move again today) and set up her new phone. Chris called, and she and the kids visited Diane today.

I don't remember discussing the events of the prior evening with Chris. I was careful to not burden the kids with such incidents. It was hard enough for them to watch what was happening to their mother, I felt

159

they didn't need to know all the incidents and details. Sometimes I would "unload" a little with a phone call to my son Don. He was a good listener, but I knew it was very difficult for him to see his mother getting worse as time went on.

2 PM Courtney from hospice was here and visited with resident and her husband. Resident expressed that there were "four people" in her room last night all asking her to do different things. Both hospice and husband were aware of the hallucinations last night and assured resident that staff is here to help her. Hospice has asked that only one staff approach, sit with, talk to, and assist resident when she is hallucinating if at all possible, and to be very calm and use a quiet, calm voice when talking to her. Her husband does not feel that the hallucinations last night are connected to the change in medication. He states that resident has had these hallucinations before when living at home. Per hospice, resident will continue on her current medications.

-- Friday, April 18, 2014 --

I met with Diane and Courtney this morning. Diane was doing pretty well but had problems telling us what might be bothering her. She couldn't get the words out, and her mouth/jaw was trembling, as well as her hands. She calmed down as I held her hand and spoke softly to her. Courtney also held her hand.

At 6:00 PM I got a call from Diane. She said "they" were going to kill her. "They" were people from Chetek with whom Diane never had contact. I told her to ask for help from the staff, and she said the staff was "in on it." This is the first sign I've seen of Capgras Syndrome regarding the staff. UGH! She hung up on me. I called Diane right back and explained that the Chetek people she was concerned about had no connections with the memory care center in Chippewa Falls where she was. After talking for several minutes, Diane said it was okay and wanted to go to bed.

5:30 PM Resident refused PM supplement of vitamin, stated, "I will not be taking that tonight. You can please leave me alone." Staff asked if she was OK, and resident stated she "hoped to be" and then shut her door on staff.

160

9:38 PM Resident refused assistance with PM cares. First attempted at 7:00PM. Asked if resident would like to get ready for bed. Resident replied, "No, I am not ready. You will just go and tell everybody and laugh at me." Tried again at 8:00 PM. Resident replied, "I'm not going. Get out of here." Tried again at 8:30 PM. Resident said, "I'm not getting ready for bed. I'm not staying here." Another staff tried also and resident refused.

Never in our life together had Diane treated people this way. It is a perfect example of how devastating Lewy Body Dementia is, completely changing the personality of its victims. Diane was a very introverted person and was always uncomfortable being in crowds but always, always polite. Prior to Lewy Bodies, she would never have treated anyone as she was treating her caregivers.

-- Saturday, April 19, 2014 --

9:14 PM Resident was hallucinating and seemed shaken. On entering resident's room, resident stated, "I just finished talking to my husband, this is why I feel like this. We always had problems even when we lived in the trailer. I have psychological problems, and he says he has all my stuff to deal with. My sickness and the bills to pay is too much." Writer is not sure if resident did indeed make a phone call to her husband. Writer was able to calm resident who went to bed early.

Here is another incident demonstrating how quickly the Lewy Body mind can change paths through the brain. When Diane called me earlier, the conversation was about my picking her up at "the church." This was very normal, as she often thought she was in a church. There was no argument or talk about Diane's "psychological problems," no talk of bills to pay, and we had never lived in a trailer. In her mind, she was causing me too much grief. Here again, no logical sense. That's the Lewy Body mind.

-- Sunday, April 20, 2014 --

We went to eat at Perkins in Eau Claire. Diane didn't seem quite as "down" as the last few days. I wonder if the meds are helping. The topic of how long the sickness lasts before she dies came up again

today. When she asked if the doctor said how long, I said, "No one knows, but it might be six to twelve months."

She replied, "That's too long."

Diane called three times between 6 and 11 PM. She's got the phone dialing down pat, and that's good. The last call was for me to come down and pick up Jim, and some kids to go somewhere.

-- Monday, April 21, 2014 --

I arrived at the memory care center at 8:45 AM. Courtney had also just arrived. She took Diane's vitals and asked how things were going. Diane feels like she is required to do all the activities, but she doesn't like playing cards and some of the other activities. We explained that she didn't have to go to the activities, the staff just invites her to come. She is having slow speech and stuttering problems regularly when talking about things that make her nervous.

-- Wednesday, April 23, 2014 --

Diane called around 6:00 PM. We had a chat, and she seemed to be doing OK. She is so paranoid over construction work at her place and kids being left alone.

Quite often Diane would tell me about the pounding next door, that there was remodeling being done on the room. She had visual perspective problems trying to figure out the 45-degree angle her bathroom door made with respect to the other walls in the room. The remodeling was going to correct that. She would often think there were large holes being made in her wall. She didn't like that because the person in the next room could see everything she was doing in her room. We would often talk on the phone about how she would like the room to look and what color the walls should be.

8:34 PM Resident refused activities. Resident did come to dinner but then got up and left before food came stating, "I'm not going to sit at that table while they talk about tits. This is a church, and we are to have

162

a nice meal, not talk about tits." This writer reassured her that we can move her to a different table so she can eat.

Upon walking into resident's room, resident told me to "be quiet the kids are asleep." Staff observed that blankets were rolled up as if someone had been sleeping in them. Staff whispered, "Okay, I'll be quiet. But we should get ready for bed." Resident was then assisted with cares. Resident is currently in room still awake.

Diane's mind seemed to cause her to see and be with children often. This is no surprise, as she always loved children, holding them and watching them play. This is a trait I can remember from her high school days, which I'm sure stems from her being the middle child in a family of six children. It was always easier to communicate with Diane when talking about children. We would talk about taking proper care of children, what the children were doing, the kind of clothes the children were wearing. It was always interesting to try to find out whose children Lewy Bodies were making her see. Sometimes she could even tell me what they were saying.

-- Thursday, April 24, 2014 --

In the afternoon, I went to the memory care center. Chris and the kids were coming over also. Trying to visit with Diane while caring for two little ones is getting to be more than Chris can handle. We had a good visit. Little Gwen wanted to go on "adventures" by walking all over the place. She really enjoys stopping at the activity room to listen to music and "dance" to the tunes. Little Reuben slept during the first part of the visit. When he woke up he walked with me around the large room outside Diane's room and down the long hall and back. He should sleep well tonight.

After Chris left, Diane was a little down. She has a tough time realizing she has been at the care center for two months. She wonders why nobody ever told her about coming there.

It was always a "downer" for me when Diane could not remember where she was or how long she was at a given place. I never knew from day to day where she thought she was. Most of the time she thought she was at

163

a church, funeral home, scout camp, or a school. Yet, when I asked one time if she could take me on a tour of the church, she said she couldn't because she didn't know where the main entrance was.

-- Friday, April 25, 2014 --

Diane is starting to have stiffness in her left hip area. She said her leg "kind of shook" yesterday when she stopped to work out the stiffness.

Diane had mentioned to me on a couple of previous walks that her hip was stiff, but it didn't seem to bother her to walk a considerable distance. I'm sure when she referred to her leg shaking it was tremors from the Parkinson's Disease. When she mentioned this I immediately thought of the time she fell at the house because her leg "didn't work right."

10:12 PM Late entry; Resident was very weak today, and her mouth was quivering. Hospice was here and stayed with her until anxiety had subsided.

-- Saturday, April 26, 2014 --

This morning I slept late. I brought the medicines Diane could no longer use to the police department. It was more than $350 worth of drugs wasted.

I got to Diane a little after 10 AM. She was in good spirits. But shortly after I got home she called and was upset that nobody was there to pick her up at the middle school. I asked her to stay there and I would be back to see her in the morning. She reluctantly agreed to do that. I've tried to call this evening but no answer. She must be walking around or at an activity.

8 AM Resident ate well and has her husband here with her now. Resident went outside for a walk with her husband. Resident came to staff crying and stated that someone had died and that we need to file some paperwork for her. She also stated that we would need to call someone to pick her up. Staff stated we would take care of it and resident went back to room.

7:27 PM Resident has been having hallucinations all PM shift and wandering a lot. Resident has also accused staff and other residents of trying to harm her. Resident has been wandering the halls and standing by the front door waiting to get out. Resident refused to eat any supper stating, "You all are trying to kill me! I will not come near any of you." Resident refused assistance from staff. Resident will not let staff touch her colostomy bag. Staff will continue to try and redirect the resident. Resident has been on 15-minute checks this shift.

-- Sunday, April 27, 2014 --

I got down to Diane's around 9:30 AM. She was sitting in the large room outside her room with her head bowed and hands folded. She told the attendant that she was talking to God. I have no doubts that that was true.

We sat for a while watching a church service on TV. She said there were people here for the funeral in her room so didn't want to go there. After a few minutes we walked over to her room and looked at the Sunday paper together.

Diane mentioned that her left leg kind of stopped working while walking in the building. She said that happened a few days ago also. I don't know if there were two instances or just one that she remembers.

-- Monday, April 28, 2014 --

We had a good visit with Courtney and talked about Diane's left leg giving out on a walk. That actually happened when Courtney and I were walking with Diane. Courtney will have the physical therapist stop by and see what she thinks.

9:26 AM Resident was assisted with AM cares this morning. She was smiling with staff. Resident also walked the hallways a lot this morning. She is currently visiting with her husband.

Whenever I read the memory care notes and saw that Diane was smiling it gave me a lift. It is gratifying to know she had some days when she related to the staff and even smiled.

165

6 PM Resident refused to go to dinner. Resident did attend bingo. Resident started to experience things about children being shot. Resident was given medication.

-- Tuesday, April 29, 2014 --

Diane called around 4:00 PM while I was working on the computer. She was afraid of two principals from the school who were going to "question" her. She thought she was in a school. She was crying, and while trying to calm her down I also broke down. Needless to say we couldn't talk for a while. She put the phone down to look at the bird feeder outside her window. When she picked up the phone again she had the earpiece and mouthpiece reversed. I hung up, and we finally got back together after she dialed me. UGH!

-- Wednesday, April 30, 2014 --

When I got to Diane's, the staff met me in the hall. Diane was having a bad morning. She was very anxious and thinking someone was going to kill her. They had given her some meds to calm her down. She was a little better when I got to the room.

The visit was difficult this morning because nothing made any sense. Diane was all over the place in conversation. When I first started talking she hushed me, not wanting the people outside to hear what I was saying. She didn't want anyone to see that she had the TV remote in her hand under her blanket in the chair.

At this stage in Diane's dementia there was a consistent theme of someone trying to kill her. After the emotional phone call the evening before and feeling she was doing pretty well, this morning was another "regression." The paranoia was quite prevalent. Her asking me to whisper so "they" couldn't hear returned. I helped her hide the TV remote a little better so it was totally invisible. I also continued to whisper. Each time she heard someone talking outside the room she would ask me what they were saying about us. I whispered to her that they were talking about some medications and weren't talking about us.

166

5:25 AM Resident is worried about not making it to school by 6 to sub for her mother today. Resident stated she just feels sick about it and is crying. Resident and writer talked for a few minutes in her room. She did calm down a bit. She is currently in her room trying to get some more rest.

9:23 AM Resident asked staff when her ride would be here to go to the center to spend the remainder of her life there. Staff sat with resident for a bit and calmed her down.

9:27 AM Resident received Lorazepam for anxiety. Resident was in her room sitting in her rocking chair, trembling and stating that she could hear lots of people talking. She asked this writer if there was a party. This writer explained that there was breakfast going on in the dining room and offered assistance in going to the dining room. Resident stated that she was not hungry. This writer sat with resident for ten minutes engaging in a small conversation, and it appeared as though resident enjoyed this. When this writer left the room resident was sitting in her rocking chair with her feet up watching the Today *show. Husband is currently in resident's room with her at this time.*

10:06 PM Resident attended activity. Resident complained about her left leg hurting.

Starting a third month

-- Thursday, May 1, 2014 --

I arrived at the memory care center at 9:30 AM. Diane was doing quite well today. There seemed to be a lot less tearfulness. We had a good visit. She hugged me for a long time when I got there.

A huge relief came in the mail today: Diane's long-term care was approved and a payment to our checking account was set up. I was so afraid there would be some kind of loop hole I didn't know about. Thanks be to God!

2:25 PM Resident was crying when she woke up, said she was scared, confused, didn't know where she was or why she was there. Staff explained to her where she was, that she was here to get help whenever she needs it and assured her that her husband would be in to visit her today.

-- Friday, May 2, 2014 --

11:03 AM Resident was actively exit seeking and pacing. Staff offered resident a change in atmosphere by walking to the bistro. Staff offered to paint resident's nails and also offered to read a book to resident. Resident given Lorazepam at 10:53 AM.

10:16 PM Resident has refused PM cares at this point. First approached at 7:30. and said, "It is time to get ready for bed." Resident replied, "No, I don't want to." Writer kept talking and resident said, "I just want to be left alone." Re-approached at 9 and resident refused to get up out of her chair. Tried again at 9:30 and resident again refused to get out of her chair. Another attempt and resident refused to get up. Resident has also refused to have her colostomy bag emptied. Continue to approach her until end of shift.

-- Saturday, May 3, 2104 --

I met Diane as she was walking down the hall this morning. She

wasn't very happy and didn't want to give me a hug. She was talking about the people who she thinks are dealing drugs and cigarettes.

We walked down to her room and visited for a while. Diane couldn't understand where she was. We went for a walk down the road. All during the walk Diane was talking about police coming to pick up some people and ambulances coming to take people who had fallen to the hospital.

One of the telltale signs Diane was having a bad day or in a bad mood was the lack of a hug when I arrived for a visit. I remember walking with her this day because she was relentless in her accounts of police and ambulances. We usually walked for half an hour, and she rarely kept on a subject for more than a few minutes. But this day I had a hard time "getting into her mind" to hold a conversation about ambulances and people who had fallen. I remember being mentally exhausted at the end of this particular walk.

Diane called around 10:15 PM. She was very confused. I couldn't understand what she was trying to say but finally got her to go to bed and sleep.

7:10 PM Resident thought staff were talking about her and refused to eat dinner and is in her room.

8:00 PM Resident received Lorazepam this evening due to insecurity and hallucinations. Interventions tried include one-on-one with staff, offering snack/meal, and going for a walk. All of these were ineffective. Resident did originally come to the dining room for dinner but left as soon as the food was served. When asked if she would like something else she stated, "You sure as hell know I do not." At this time resident is now calm. Resident took all other medications well. No further concerns at this time.

There were many instances of Diane's dementia causing her to respond or behave belligerently. This is another example of how caring the staff was toward Diane. There was an excellent understanding of how dementia causes residents to say and do things they were once incapable

169

of doing. It didn't matter what Diane did or said, the staff always treated her with respect and kindness. This was a major comfort for me.

-- Sunday, May 4, 2014 --

We had a May birthday party and took family photos at the memory center today. When I got there around 10 AM, Diane's room was a little messy. She had called me earlier very confused and crying. She was OK after talking with me for a while. She went down with a staff member to get a little breakfast. I picked up the room and laid out clothes for her to wear during the photo session.

We had a good day--grandkids opening presents, family photos taken, cake, ice cream, and I played music with Mike and his brother Dave.

Diane was pretty tired after the long day. Love her much.

8:00 AM Resident received Lorazepam at 10:30 AM. Resident was pacing the halls, hallucinating, believing that other residents and staff wanted to blow up the facility. Resident was also hiding in the A dining room. Resident would not take the Lorazepam for this writer but did take it for another staff member. That staff member then did one on one visit with resident and took her for a walk in the courtyard. Resident appeared to be calm and smiling. Lorazepam was effective.

11:09 AM Resident refused cares and was hallucinating. Writer was able to calm her down and get her smiling again. Resident also spoke to husband, and that helped as well. Writer spent time with her in the courtyard, and she enjoyed it. Writer will get her dressed and ready for company after lunch. At this time resident is in her room relaxing. Resident seemed to have recovered from her anxiety.

6:12 PM Upon coming to A quad at 3:00 PM resident's family was having a birthday party. Resident appeared happy and to be having a good time. Resident's family thought they lost a checkbook during party but it was found in a bag they had. Resident ate well for dinner and attended movie night in living room.

Family photo taken on May 4, 2014

Front row, left to right: Gwenyth Rambo, Jim Adams, Diane
Adams, Addy Adams; back row, left to right: Becca Adams,
Taylor Adams, Chris Rambo, Reuben Rambo, Mike Rambo,
Greg Adams, Laurie Adams, Don Adams, Heidi Adams

Diane did very well once the kids and grandchildren arrived. Everyone
visited, and the grandkids played with the toys we had in Diane's room. I
remember Diane smiling a lot when talking with the kids. She loved
watching the smaller grandchildren scoot around the room. After taking
the photos we all gathered in the food service area to have birthday cake
for Gwenyth and Reuben. Diane seemed to be enjoying the party. Once
in a while a resident would stop by to see what was going on,
particularly during the time we were playing music.

-- Monday, May 5, 2014 --

Today's was a very mentally draining visit. During the 2 1/2 hours with Diane there wasn't any sensible conversation. We went from being at her childhood neighbor's farm house, to seeing people on the bed and in the closet door, to not having car keys, to needing money to pay for food, to not being able to go home. It was nearly impossible to get inside her head and carry out a conversation. I can see significant change in cognitive response and ability during the last few visits.

-- Wednesday, May 7, 2014 --

I arrived at the memory center at 9:00 AM. Diane was just getting ready for our trip to Chetek. We stopped by the house for a while. I went to take the garbage can back, and Diane went into the house. When I came back into the house Diane had walked into the bedroom area. I met her in the hallway. She said I had things in pretty good order and then leaned against the bedroom doorway crying. I held her in my arms, and she said she missed the house and me. I couldn't help but cry also.

I was devastated by Diane's comments about me and our home. It was one of the times when her brain evidently caused the right paths to be accessed as she remembered the house and missed it. Diane never said anything about missing me when I visited her at the memory center, but when she associated the house with me, she missed me. It was gratifying to know that she missed me. Lord knows how much I missed Diane.

3:08 PM Resident appears to be walking with a slight limp in left leg. Resident told staff she does not feel any sort of pain. Staff looked over resident's leg, and there are no visible marks. Resident said that this tends to happen after sitting for a long period of time. Resident said this will get better after walking. Staff relayed the message to night crew and will pay close attention.

-- Thursday, May 8, 2014 --

9:51 PM Resident stayed in her room most of the evening. She did come out for dinner and would sometimes step outside her door, get frustrated

172

at staff, and then go back into her room. Resident was hallucinating about a baby being in her room and was angry at staff that they were not taking care of it. Staff tried to reassure her that they were taking care of it, but resident would say, "Yeah, that's what they all say." Medication was attempted because resident continued to seem agitated. Resident refused and seemed to remain calm so was not attempted again.

-- Friday, May 9, 2014 --

Diane called at 6:15 PM. She was just wondering how I was doing as she hadn't heard from me. We chatted a while and she was wanting to go to bed. It is gratifying to know that she still knows me and wonders how I'm doing. So far at the memory center and my half-day visits there has been no evidence of Capgras Syndrome and seeing more than one Jim Adams.

As difficult as it was to transfer Diane to the memory care center, I was always "her Jim" when I visited. Words cannot express what this meant to me. She no longer feared me and would give me a hug when I saw her. Diane would know me as her husband, and I could mention the children and grandchildren without her telling me I was a spy trying to take over and steal the house or money. Even when she could not make sense of what she was seeing outside, or couldn't think logically, she seemed to accept what I would say in my efforts to try to "get inside" her mind when we conversed.

-- Saturday, May 10, 2014 --

Diane and I had a very good visit and conversation was quite normal.

Don came to the house in the afternoon while Becca was swimming with Addy and her friends in Rice Lake. We talked about where I might want to live as time goes on, a good question that I've really never thought about.

When Don visited, he would cause me to think about things that never entered my mind. I was always thinking about Diane and caring for her and didn't take time to think about my life. I told Don I hadn't given it

173

much thought, but wherever I lived, there would have to be a good shop area where I could spend time building model planes and doing wood projects.

-- Sunday, May 11, 2014 --

Diane called at midnight last night. She was confused about where she was and very concerned about babysitting the little ones, meaning Gwenyth and Reuben. I talked with her for 15 minutes until she agreed to go to bed. I assured her I would see her in the morning.

When calls like this came from Diane, it was always difficult to get back to sleep. Each time I would shed tears of deep sorrow for her. I often wished I could just instantaneously be beamed to her side so I could hold her and comfort her.

Arriving at Diane's I found her in a "down" state. She was teary eyed and not understanding what was happening. I just listened for a long time holding her hand. I was able to get her to think about the birthday party last Sunday.

We went for another long walk. Our conversation often involves what I'm doing. She still believes I'm working full time. She asked me this morning if I was seeing anyone else. She was relieved when I said, "Absolutely not."

3:31 PM Late Entry for 5/10/14: 4PM - 8PM Resident spent most of the evening in her room. She refused dinner stating that she wasn't hungry and also that staff was trying to kill her. Staff left resident's room and came back after dinner to check on her. She did not mention anything about staff trying to kill her, but she still did not want to eat. She spent the remainder of the evening in her room.

7:56 PM Resident was crying in her room for an hour. Talked with her for some time. Resident calmed down.

174

-- Monday, May 12, 2014 --

It's 12:40 PM and I just got back from seeing Diane. She was really "down" this morning. She was on her way back from morning exercise with Courtney the hospice nurse when I approached her and gave her a hug. She was trembling in the hands and lips as she talked. This seems to happen when she is nervous about things. Courtney checked Diane out, and physically things are OK.

It hurt deep in my soul to see Diane tremble. She had no control of her trembling hands or lips and because of this words just wouldn't come out right, frustrating her. I always felt depressed when this happened. There was nothing I could do to help but hold her hand, hug her, or be close to her until the trembling ceased and she was able to form words again. Usually within a few minutes she would be back to a more normal state and we could go for a walk or I could redirect her in some way.

-- Tuesday, May 13, 2014 --

I arrived at Diane's around 12:45 PM. She was sitting in her chair with tears in her eyes. She was feeling "down" again. We talked for a long time. I mostly just listened. The conversation went from Diane hitting someone with her car last night, worries of police action and court appearances, to concern about what I was going to do about the cows and chickens at the farm.

Today was a most difficult day, mentally. The ride home was long. It is extremely painful to see someone you love so much lose their mental capacity to a disease like Lewy Body Dementia with Parkinson's.

12:59 PM Resident was crying when staff went in to wake her. Staff asked what was wrong and she said she was "crazy." Staff comforted her and got her all prettied up for the day. She said she felt much better after resident went to exercises and watched I love Lucy *in the bistro. No concerns.*

-- Wednesday, May 14, 2014 --

I arrived at the memory center at 9:30 AM. Diane was walking by the entrance as I came in. She was finishing a walk with Courtney the hospice nurse. Diane told Courtney about everybody wanting to know about her ostomy. She said sometimes they don't want to change or clean out her pouch. Diane said, "One day I just asked them how they would feel if they had to put up with a bag of shit hanging on them." I guess they agreed with her.

It was so uncharacteristic of Diane to say something like "bag of shit," yet it was such a profound statement. Sometimes humor results from the seemingly random pathways the brain takes with dementia, and such an incident lightened things up for both the hospice nurse and me. Diane was smiling as she told us about this incident, and I think she was fully aware of the humor in the story.

10:13 AM This writer met with POA/Husband (Jim) and Hospice RN Courtney for a 30-day care conference. Writer discussed anxious behaviors with daily hallucinations, crying, and that reassurance from staff and approaching resident in calm voice and having one-on-one with resident almost always helps. On occasion use of Lorazepam has been needed due to interventions being ineffective, and the meds have always been effective. At this time, all of us agreed that using the Lorazepam as needed is what would be best.

Husband did note that he receives between 2-3 calls throughout the day from wife but does not mind. (She has an in-room phone that he has set up with his number on speed dial). She is currently in the process of changing antidepressants and increasing her dosage. Husband, hospice and I have agreed that so far the change has been positive. We will continue to monitor.

Resident continues to toilet self with no signs of incontinence or concerns. Resident colostomy site has stayed looking healthy with no concerns with stoma. Staff continues to empty the bag twice a day and as needed.

Resident is on general diet and had good intakes. Resident's weight has been stable. A dietician will be out next week to assess resident due to complaint of lumpy feeling in throat when swallowing. Vitals and weight have remained stable.

Resident will almost always attend activities with staff encouragement/reassurance. There were no other concerns.

POA stated he was very happy with the care and how much improvement she has shown with behaviors and her depression since arriving.

-- Thursday, May 15, 2014 --

I arrived at the memory care center at 9:30 AM. One of the staff met me at the door. She told me there were issues with Diane this morning. I sat down to talk with Diane. The issues revolved around all the spy cameras and microphones in the place. Diane didn't want me to talk for fear of being heard.

It's about 1:45 PM. Diane just called and was in a very agitated mood. She insisted I "get over here" and get our kids out of there or they will go to jail. Everyone there was against her--I need to call "111" to get the cops there. She hung up on me when I tried to explain that no one there can have a gun. I called the center to see if they could check on Diane and re-direct her or try some of the meds that might calm her down. UGH!

The paranoia of Capgras Syndrome was perhaps the most difficult symptom to help Diane overcome. It would persist for long periods of time and usually involved our kids, cops, court appearances, spy equipment placed in the facility or her room, and thoughts of someone wanting to kill her. In many ways, the staff had taken the place of the various "Jims" when Diane was at the house. The staff became the bad guys, which was totally understandable because they were visible 24 hours per day.

2:13 PM Resident requested to have her colostomy bag changed. When staff entered residents room and showed resident the colostomy bag

177

explaining that staff was going to change her bag for her, resident said, "Oh that's what you're calling it." Staff said, "You don't want me to change your bag for you?" Resident said, "No." Staff left resident's room and entered the medication room. A few minutes later resident came to the medication room and opened the door and asked, "How many of you does it take?" Staff attempted to explain to resident that writer was only trying to help her. Resident then kicked the door. Writer offered alone time, one-on-one time, and brought resident fresh ice water. All attempts to redirect were unsuccessful. Writer approached another staff to attempt to give Lorazepam, which was also unsuccessful. Resident is currently in her room and continues to pull the door, holding it shut, when writer knocks on the door. Staff will continue to monitor and will pass this on to the next shift.

3:47 PM Writer continued to observe resident as requested by AM staff. Resident's brother came and visited with resident. Resident received Lorazepam and it was effective.

-- Friday, May 16, 2014 --

I haven't had a call from Diane today so I hope she is doing OK.

10:34 AM This morning when staff went in to assist resident with her shower, she had a bag full of loose stool. This writer had her sit down to drain it, and got her into the shower where this writer realized the loose stool just kept coming out, filling the bag for a second time. This writer then realized that resident had a softball size hard lump sticking out of her stomach. Staff notified another to look at it, and she also stated that it was very large and to call hospice. This writer notified hospice and the on-call nurse (Courtney). When nurse called back she stated she was not worried, as this has been there since the resident was at home. Resident's doctor has seen it and is not concerned. Hospice nurse then came to visit and stated it was a little larger than a month ago and will contact the doctor again to see what she thought.

-- Saturday May 17, 2014 --

I visited Diane this afternoon and she was still feeling quite depressed. We walked for a half an hour and sat in the chairs outside the center

178

for another half an hour. There is much paranoia over the staff and cameras and recorders. There seems to be no recollection of day and time now. Short-term memory seems almost gone.

Diane called a little after 7:00 PM, mad at me for not telling her there were four other people sleeping in her room. I was able to convince her that she was alone and it was OK to sleep there in her bed.

9:39 AM Resident appeared very wobbly when walking and heard her left knee clicking as she walked. Resident's exercises were performed this morning but resident has to use this writer for balance most of the time. Resident appears upset at this time. Resident has tears in her eyes but told writer nothing was wrong. Reminded her that her husband would be here soon. This appeared to make her a little happier. Resident requested to eat breakfast in her room and only wanted fruit and toast. Will continue to monitor resident throughout shift.

5:49 PM Resident took all medications well this evening. Resident was escorted to dinner by staff. She was seated at a table; just before being served she sat up from the table attempting to leave. Staff was able to redirect resident into staying at the dinner table and served her food. She sat at the table for a minute, never touching her food or plate and stood up from the table again. She stated, "I didn't ask for cold food." Staff offered to warm her food for her. She rolled her eyes and left the quad. She received fresh water in her bedroom at 9:30 PM tonight. Resident was fully assisted with all PM cares including the emptying/cleaning of her colostomy bag. No further concerns at this time.

It is disheartening for me to learn that Diane wasn't eating. It's not that her body didn't need food, the dementia had taken a pathway in the brain that caused her to refuse food or services being provided. There is nothing the caretakers could do. Her brain did not respond to kindness, offers of help, or any other caregiving intervention. If Diane were to be forced to eat something she would no doubt feel threatened and may even have become violent.

-- Sunday, May 18, 2014 --

When I got to the memory center, I couldn't find Diane in her normal area of the facility. I walked around the large square and found her sitting in a recliner. She was slumped over with her head tilted to one side, so typical of what one would expect to see in a memory care center. I walked up to her. She opened her eyes, put her finger to her nose, and said I shouldn't talk as "they" were listening. She was paranoid about the staff and most everyone else.

We went for a ride through Irvine Park in Chippewa Falls. As we were driving through the park, we saw Don and Taylor. Their church was doing an annual clean-up session at the park. I think Diane enjoyed the ride.

Whenever Diane agreed to go for a ride, I liked to take her to Irvine Park. There was always a lot of brain stimulation in the form of ducks and geese, animals in the small zoo, and easy walking paths. Diane immediately knew Don and Taylor when we saw them. We chatted for a while along the road before the two of them had to go help with park clean up. Diane sat quietly and enjoyed hearing our conversation. When we got out of the car and walked to the duck pond, Diane was very unsteady and didn't want to stay long.

Diane called three times in less than an hour today. She was worried that she was not caring for "the kids." She also didn't know where she was or where I was. She thought she was at Samuelsons' farm and I was in Hixton. Samuelsons were her neighbors when she was growing up, and Hixton is my hometown, about seven miles away.

11:01 AM When staff was trying to wake her, resident kept repeating, "What did they do to me?" Staff reassured her that no one wanted to do anything to her and that writer was there to help her get dressed and ready for breakfast.

6:49 PM Resident appeared anxious and depressed late afternoon. Resident was taken to the courtyard for activities and enjoyed the story telling. Resident also stood by the front door waiting to see if she could get out--please keep close watch. Resident had dinner and is now in living room watching a movie with other residents.

9:57 PM Lorazepam was given at 3:45 PM for exit-seeking and hallucinations and was effective.

-- Monday, May 19, 2014 --

Diane was having a tough morning. She was quite depressed. Courtney, the hospice nurse, was there to see how Diane was doing. Diane didn't make any sense at all when she talked--more paranoia and no understanding of where she was.

There appears to be significant swelling around Diane's stoma and the intestines surrounding it. She doesn't have any pain. I'm wondering if her colon cancer has returned, as if Lewy Body Dementia with Parkinson's isn't enough.

Throughout Diane's entire ordeal I always worried that her cancer might return. The area around the stoma felt hard and was larger than my fist. I always felt that bodily stress influenced Diane's dementia behaviors. If the cancer had indeed returned I wondered what it might do to her behavior and outlook. It seemed so unfair that she had Lewy Body Dementia with Parkinson's Disease and now her cancer had possibly returned.

It's not easy to leave Diane at the center when she is so depressed. Another teary-eyed drive back to Chetek.

During the drive home I was grieving so deeply for Diane I couldn't hold back my tears. But, as I went along the highway, I began to think about what Diane had always said about "things taking too long." We had both prayed constantly that God would take Diane sooner rather than later and that her suffering would be minimal. I began to wonder if God wasn't accelerating things through her cancer. I recalled how fast the Lewy Body and Parkinson's had moved in a period of a few months. If cancer were added, Diane's "going home" would come very rapidly. The thought of Diane suffering for a lesser amount of time came with the awful realization that she soon wouldn't be with me at all.

181

9:07 AM Resident was in a crying kind of a mood today. Her husband reported that she has been this way since he arrived. Hospice was here to evaluate her swallowing and didn't seem to find any changes at this time.

2:27 PM Lorazepam given at 12:30 PM when interventions were ineffective. She had time with family, walked the building, had one-on-one time with staff, quiet time, and food was offered. Nothing seemed to help her stop crying. Lorazepam was effective.

10:28 PM Resident has refused all PM cares. Resident has been by the front doors and has refused to get up out of the chair.

-- Tuesday, May 20, 2014 --

When I got to the memory care center Diane was not doing well. She was depressed and quite teary-eyed.

After visiting for a while we went for a walk. It was windy outside and a little cool, but Diane really likes getting out in the fresh air.

As we walked, Diane talked continuously but made little sense. She seems to be getting more incoherent at time goes by.
She didn't want to go to noon lunch today. I started to walk her down to the lunch area and she stopped and started to cry. I took her back to her room, and she ate her lunch there.

10:44 PM Resident took medications after several attempts. She was given Lorazepam at 7:30 PM; this was effective. Behaviors causing medication to be given include throwing water at staff, insecurities due to hallucinations, and excessive pacing/wandering. Attempted interventions include one-on-one staff (resident unwilling), offering snack/meal, and spending time with other residents. All attempts at intervention were ineffective. Resident has refused all PM cares for this writer. She did allow this writer to physically look at her ostomy bag but would not allow staff to help her empty/clean bag. Resident continues to appear restless/agitated. No further concerns at this time.

-- Wednesday, May 21, 2014 --

I got down to the memory center about 9:20 AM. Courtney, the hospice nurse, was with Diane. It was another rough night for Diane, she had packed her things for a move again. Courtney put most of the things back.

Diane's depression seemed to be heightened, and there seemed to be less and less "good" pathways the brain was taking in daily thought processes. It was a blessing to have Courtney to talk with. After she checked Diane over, Courtney and I would often go out to the living room area and talk about the changes we saw from week to week. We were both quite amazed at how fast the Lewy Body Dementia and Parkinson's Disease seemed to be progressing. We also talked about the possibility of Diane's cancer returning.

Diane called twice this evening. I couldn't understand anything she was saying. I just listened and tried to put myself in her mind so we could somewhat communicate.

2:42 PM Resident was wandering the halls. She stopped at the front entry and looked outside. Staff asked if she was OK, and she replied, "No. Are you the one who is going to shoot me?" She then walked away from staff.

9:51 PM Resident was given a Lorazepam for anxiety. Resident was offered food, activities and to use the bathroom. Resident was walking the halls telling staff that they should not do things, that we were all in trouble for what we had done. Resident refused to be assisted to the toilet but allowed staff to assist her with other cares. Medication was effective.

-- Thursday, May 22, 2014 --

Jack, Connie, and I arrived at the memory center about 10:00 AM. I found Diane slumped in her chair sleeping. I put my hand on her head, and she slowly opened her eyes. She was very disoriented, and her voice was slow and slurred. I couldn't make out what she was saying. It was like she was on drugs or drunk. I finally got her up, but she was very unsteady on her feet. We went out to the fireplace room to visit with Jack and Connie. She would keep whispering in my ear that we need to be careful, as she wasn't sure of what's going on in this place.

Norma and Cleo came for a visit at 10:30 AM. We all had a good visit and Diane was happy to see her sisters.

This was a relatively good day for Diane. She listened to the many different conversations, smiled, and sometimes laughed at some of the humorous stories being shared. She always loved it when her sisters and brother Mel came to visit. To have Jack and Connie there at the same time seemed to make her happy. Diane didn't talk much during the visit but did respond when spoken to. It was painfully apparent to everyone that she was unable to carry on a logical conversation. As I listened and watched Diane respond, I was impressed with how everyone responded to the situation in such a positive and very normal way, as if there was nothing wrong. Diane was always very quiet during family gatherings, and everyone knew that was the way she was. This day was no different. Diane and I had such wonderful family supporting us during this time.

7:05 PM Resident has been anxious, talking about hiking out of the facility. Resident called husband and left a message. Asked all quads to help keep an eye out so resident does not leave the building. Resident is hanging out by the foyer at this time.

11:00 PM Resident took all medications well this evening. She received Lorazepam at 9:30 PM. Behaviors were wanting to go home and insecurity due to hallucinations. Resident was pacing the hall yelling, "Is anyone going to help me get out of this hospital? I am certainly not staying here!" This writer explained to her that we are not a hospital but assisted living. Writer explained what we do here and why she is here. Resident did allow staff to enter her bedroom with her. She was stuttering a lot and appeared to be fumbling for words. She was very upset, as she believed the male residents in the facility were selling drugs and she would be the victim of a drug deal gone bad. Staff attempted to calmly explain to her these were only her housemates and that the facility is very safe. This did not appear to help. Interventions attempted included offering a snack, going for a walk, and one-on-one time with staff. These were all ineffective. The medication was effective as resident later allowed staff to assist her with PM cares. No further concerns at this time.

It was easy for me to understand Diane's brain getting confused over family-associated events; however, the reference to drugs and drug deals continued to puzzle me. I don't ever recall having any discussions about drugs. The only possibility I can think of is television. I'm sure some of the programs we watched over the years involved shows with drug trafficking themes. The dementia must have been causing some of those stored memories to be accessed and put together in ways that made her believe she was involved in some sort of drug-dealing facility. Such misdirected memory paths made "getting inside" Diane's mind even more difficult. It's like the brain tried to put together logical connections between memories but couldn't relate the memories to time and circumstances.

-- Friday, May 23, 2014 --

This is the last Friday session with the math teachers in Birchwood. The day went very well, and I got to come home an hour early.

Working with the teachers gave me a break from the caretaking role. There were times when it was hard to put everything I had into working with the teaching staff. The times when Diane called and was confused or needed help with the TV remote were particularly trying. The teaching staff knew about Diane and were extremely supportive and understanding.

6:12 AM Around 5:00 AM resident was knocking on the inside of her door. When I opened the door she asked if there was a flood or something happening with water because she could hear it splashing everywhere. I reassured her there was no flood and there was nothing to worry about. She said, "Thank you," and closed the door.

10:20 AM Resident was having hallucinations about seeing dead bodies in her room. This writer approached resident to offer her a shower this AM. Resident refused three times. Staff will try to approach her after lunch.

10:28 PM Writer was sitting at the nurse's station when writer heard a noise and saw a chair pushed into the wall in the doorway to the living room and resident's legs on the floor. Writer went to resident and asked what happened. Resident stated she missed the chair. Vitals done and motion test completed. Skin assessment done. No complaints of pain. No new skin issues. Fifteen minute checks already in place.

-- Saturday, May 24, 2014 --

This was not a good day for Diane. I arrived at the memory center at 9:30AM. Diane was refusing to get up, get dressed, and have breakfast. She was incoherent over people trying to kill her and not making sense. I just sat on the bed and listened to her for a while and finally convinced her to sit up. After talking for a while she was willing to let someone help her take a shower and get dressed. It took about 45 minutes to get her out of bed. We had a good walk and visit until noon lunch was being served. She didn't want me to leave. It is extremely difficult to leave her with tears in her eyes. I'm so afraid if I start staying longer the Capgras Syndrome involving the other Jims will come back.

There were many days when I didn't want to leave Diane. Still, I could see symptoms of Capgras Syndrome happening to the staff at the memory center and didn't want that to happen again with me. Diane didn't need to fear me. She already had too many other fears.

9:46 PM Resident refused to come down for dinner. She walked the halls and tried getting out the front door. She was worried that there were animals hiding in her room.

Diane's Lewy Body brain seemed to generate connections to animals. When she was home animals would appear in the bedroom, but she was never afraid of them. She just seemed to accept the fact they appeared and disappeared. To her they were harmless creatures. Now, a few months later, she was afraid of animals in her room and wanted to get out of the memory care center.

-- Sunday, May 25, 2014 --

I arrived at the memory center at 9:30 AM. One of the staff members again met me in the hall and said Diane was not in a good state. She had refused to take her meds, get cleaned up, and attend breakfast. She had physically attacked the staff this morning because they were "all plotting to kill her." This is the first time that Diane has become violent. She had hidden around the corner of a room, and as the staff members came by she jumped out and began swinging at them. They got her calmed down and sat her by herself in one of the large rooms. That is where I found her. She wouldn't let me touch her and thought "they" had me on their side also.

She finally allowed me to take her for a long walk outside. During the entire walk Diane talked about having to take excessive drugs, murder, court appearances, and staff being against her. She had some paper wrinkled up and stuffed in her sock. She said it was five dollars. A little later she pulled it out and said it was an article about "last night's happenings."

When we got back from our walk, just prior to lunch, Tammy, a staff member, met us outside Diane's room. Diane went to her and said she was sorry and gave her a hug. WOW!

In our life together, I never witnessed Diane become violent with anybody. She was always very calm and passive regardless of the situation she found herself in. The Lewy Body Dementia had twisted her brain paths in such a manner that she felt everyone was going to kill her. I was apparently part of the plot. Her brain did the only "logical" thing the brain could do: fight back. The Capgras Syndrome also had her brain thinking that everyone, particularly the staff, was out to kill her.

When Diane gave the caretaker she swung at a hug and told her she was sorry, that brought tears to my eyes. Suddenly, Diane's brain found a reality path recalling the violent incident. She recognized Tammy as a caregiver rather than someone out to kill her. Incredible!

8:37 AM Writer arrived to work and was getting a report from previous shift employee. Resident had been hiding behind the pillar, jumped out

187

and began swinging, her arms punching at both staff. Resident stated, "I know what you did! How many of you are there?" Writer said, "I'm sorry I'm not sure what you mean. I just got here." Resident said, "I sure would like to know what was in that letter you received." Writer attempted to explain to resident that writer had just arrived to work and was not sure what was happening. Resident said, "Oh well, I guess you're going to play that game," and turned and began walking down the hallway in direction of D quad. Resident was given alone time.

10:00 AM resident's husband arrived at the facility. Writer noticed him in the hallway and approached resident who was sitting quietly in B quad living room and told resident, "I see Jim is here." Resident said, "Oh, isn't that nice." Writer then asked if resident wanted to walk with writer to see Jim and resident said, "No, he can just come to me." Writer met husband in the hallway and explained what had been taking place.

1:00 PM. Before lunch resident returned to her room with her husband. Upon returning, resident and husband approached writer. Resident's husband said resident had something to say to writer. Resident said, "I know I was mean to you today, and I am sorry." Resident asked staff for a hug. Staff gave resident a hug and told resident not to worry about it. After lunch resident approached writer and said, "I am really sorry." Again writer told resident not to worry about it.

This violent outburst demonstrates how important it was to know as many staff members as possible who were caring for the person I loved. I cannot possibly extend enough thanks for the wonderful care they gave Diane and the support they gave me.

10:25 AM When resident and this writer arrived at B dining room, resident would not enter the dining room to sit down and eat. She just kept mumbling words. She agreed to let staff take her old meds patch off, but when staff assisted putting new one on she said, "I don't need two shots." Staff reassured her that she needed her new patch. Later staff attempted to approach resident with her morning Ensure. Resident swung her arm and said, "NO! That will make me fall over and die." Staff assured her that it was a milkshake and that it was hers since she didn't eat breakfast. She stated, "No!" again and said, "Get Away." Staff then left resident to calm down.

4:34 PM Resident appears to be concerned and anxious this morning. Resident walked up to staff and stated she thought the building was going to start on fire tomorrow morning. Staff assured resident this was not the case. Resident replied by stating, "No one can be trusted in this place."

8:15 PM Resident walked the halls and spent time in her room. When staff asked her if she was ready to come down to dinner she said, "You can go ahead and shoot me. I don't give a shit anymore." Staff reassured her that that was not going to happen.

-- Monday, May 26, 2014 --

At 7:30 AM, my neighbor, Dave, picked me up and we went downtown to have breakfast together. We had a great visit; we hadn't talked in quite some time.

I had several friends and neighbors who took me out, which allowed me to learn what was going on in the "other" world. It also gave them opportunities to ask questions about how Diane was doing and how I was coping with everything. Each time I did this I felt refreshed. It was like seeing old friends after being on a long trip. There was always humor in our conversations. It felt good to laugh with them. These friends and neighbors may not know just how much their support means to me, but their friendship and caring helped me through this very rough time in my life. It was important and necessary for me to accept their help.

After breakfast with Dave I went to visit Diane. She was not doing well. She was very angry about the staff being "against" her. She threw some clothes across the bed. She wouldn't eat breakfast or take her medicine. It seems like things have turned from crying and depression to fear and anger.

Diane wouldn't let the staff help her get dressed or clean out her ostomy pouch. I sat beside her, holding her hand and putting my arm around her, and just listened and sympathized with her. While Diane was getting ready for our walk outside, I had a chance to explain to a couple of the staff members what Capgras Syndrome was and how

189

Diane behaves because of it. They knew about Lewy Body Dementia but had never heard of Capgras Syndrome.

I was impressed with the patience the young staff had with residents. It must be very hard on them, particularly when the medical profession doesn't know what causes these diseases.

-- Tuesday, May 27, 2014 -

2:18 PM When writer entered resident's room to invite resident to the afternoon activity, resident was hiding behind her chair. When asked to join in the activity resident said, "I want no part of the murders that are going on." Writer asked what resident meant by that, and resident waved her hand toward her bed and said, "Look there." Writer then took resident's quilt and lifted it in the air, showing resident that there was nothing under her quilt, that her bed was just a little messy. Resident then said, "Oh, I see," in a sarcastic tone. Writer left the room giving resident space and alone time.

8:44 PM Shift 4:30 - 8:30 PM. Resident asked to go to bed early. Resident decided to remove night gown and dress in street clothes. Resident is again walking the halls at this time.

9:00 PM Resident refused to take medications stating, "I don't trust you and the doctor didn't order them for me. I already took this medication yesterday and don't need it again today."

-- Wednesday, May 28, 2014 --

I got a call from the memory center at 9:45 PM telling me that Diane had fallen. Diane said she had "fallen down the stairs." She was OK, but it's the second fall in less than a week.

10:06 PM Writer was taking garbage to B quad and noticed resident sitting outside her bedroom door on the floor. Writer asked what happened and resident stated, "I fell down stairs." Writer took vitals and did range of motion with no complaints or concerns. Resident was assisted off the floor. Resident stated her left leg was hurting after standing. After a few steps, the pain went away and is normal for this resident. Resident was assisted back to her room. Resident stated she was dizzy before she fell down the stairs but is not feeling dizzy anymore. There are no stairs in the facility.

-- Thursday, May 29, 2014 --

When I first walked by Diane's room I couldn't find her. Then as I walked down the hall it occurred to me that the person sitting with the staff member in the dining area was Diane. I had walked right by her. She looked so different: frail, withdrawn. She just didn't look like Diane. She had a bad morning but finally got calmed down by sitting by herself. We went for a short walk and then sat outside for a while. We came inside at 10:30 AM and I read a couple of poems to her. She seemed to enjoy that. She was nodding off by 11:00 AM and I left so she could get a short nap before lunch.

I remember this day very well. There was no smile or acknowledgment of my being there. It was like Diane wasn't "in the now."

I stopped to visit with Chris for a few minutes. We had a much needed chat. Love her!

I appreciated being able to talk with Chris this day. We just talked about anything but Diane's condition. Chris could bring me back to the "real" world by talking about her Internet-based scrapbooking programs and techniques she used in lessons she puts on-line. We could talk about little Gwen and Reuben and how fast they were growing. We talked about how Reuben was learning so fast from his big sister Gwenyth. What a blessing to have my kids so close by during this time.

2 AM Resident was assisted with cares later in the morning due to refusing cares and being suspicious of staff, stating things like, "You don't need to be sneaking around my room," and calling one staff member the devil. Resident placed her ottoman in front of her door and piled clothes to block staff from entering her room. Resident's husband came in shortly after and took resident for a walk outside. Resident appears to be in better mood at this time.

7:04 PM Resident was helped with PM cares. Resident has been taking lists of phone numbers and activity sheets off of nurses' station and placing them in her bag, pointing to them while telling staff it's "all her fault" and she's "not even a relative."

-- Friday, May 30, 2014 --

I visited Diane a little after 1:00 PM. She was mad that I was late and nobody told her. She had things laid out on the bed ready to "go." We visited until 2:30 PM when the massage therapist came to give Diane a treatment. It wasn't but a few minutes and Diane was so relaxed she fell asleep. I chatted with the therapist while she worked on Diane. After an hour Diane woke up when Greg came to visit. We went for a walk before dinner. During the walk there wasn't any coherent conversation. Greg and I just listened and agreed with what she was trying to say.

What a wonderful thing to witness firsthand, the magic performed by that therapist. Diane's dementia had her so insecure, agitated, worried, and fearful most of the time it showed in her demeanor. After a couple of minutes I could see Diane's whole body relax, her eyes close, and the soft music enter her mind, displacing any dementia-instilled thoughts. I remember thinking how wonderful it would be for Diane if this could be a continuous thing. Then my mind would come back to reality and realize that dementia would, in all likelihood, cause this to be a threatening thing for Diane. The therapist would become an imposter wanting to do her harm. I guess it was better to have massage therapy only a couple times a week.

-- Saturday, May 31, 2014 --

Diane has been in the memory care center for a full three months. The long-term care policy begins to kick in June first but no payment for 30 days after that date. Insurance companies sure know how to get you to pay as much out of your pocket as possible before paying their amount. They should change the wording of their documentation to say payment starts <u>120 days after admission</u> to a facility because that is the truth. I'm thankful we have the insurance but one needs to know how much money to put away for the waiting period.

In all the years Diane and I were saving for the future, our financial advisors never brought up the subject of costs incurred before long-term insurance began payments. This is a significant amount--$25,000 to $30,000 or more--and should be considered in any financial planning. Diane and I had put away what we thought was enough to cover both of us in medical emergencies, but this, and more, was used up during the insurance waiting period.

This added another concern for me: if I became ill and required hospitalization, there would be another waiting period required, and we would have to take money from our retirement fund. With the cost of medical care today I could have easily become impoverished in a short time. (A note here: I have a flyer on the refrigerator from an insurance company stating that "72% of Americans become impoverished after one year of nursing home care." Seems to me that America has a real problem on its hands.)

Diane wasn't doing very well this morning. She had hit one of the staff on the head in the food service area. I found her sitting in the corner in her nightgown barefoot. She was very groggy and sleepy. This is the first night after starting Lorazepam. We will have to monitor this very closely, as this drug is not recommended for Lewy Body Dementia, particularly in large doses. It took an hour to get Diane going. She is pretty incontinent now, often not making it to the bathroom.

When we changed Diane's medicine, I always used the Internet to check for side effects. Every drug seemed to have undesirable side effects, but for dementia patients the effects could be devastating. Yet, there often comes a time when desperation descends and almost anything is worth trying. Seeing Diane in such fear and anxiety so often was reason enough to change medicines.

8:40 AM Staff went into resident's room at 7:15 AM to wake her for cares and breakfast. She got out of bed and walked out into the hall. Resident stated, "I know what you're up to, and I'm not staying in here!" Staff assured her that we just wanted to help her get dressed so she could eat. She again stated, "You act all nice so you can give me the poison!" She then proceeded to walk the halls on every quad in her nightgown. She told a staff member that she was planning on lighting a

193

fire in here and walked around gathering paper and tearing it into pieces. A staff member was sitting at the dining room table socializing with residents at breakfast, and this resident walked up to her from behind and slapped and pushed her on the back of the head. All staff are made aware of her agitation and told to keep an eye on her and keep her safe.

8:33 PM Resident refused to be assisted with all cares saying, "No. Get away from me. I am not going there." Writer approached three times and another staff also approached.

10:19 PM Resident took all medications this evening. However, staff had to make several attempts before being successful. She received scheduled Lorazepam, which has been ineffective. Resident has continued to pace excessively as well as hallucinate. This evening she has been talking to a blanket she believes to be a little girl. She has been rearranging the living room furniture, stating she is moving out, and has been rearranging dining room chairs into a circle, placing a plant in the middle of the circle and speaking to it.

Month four, getting worse fast

-- Sunday, June 1, 2014 --

Diane was just finishing a shower and getting dressed when I arrived at the memory center today. We sat in the room for a while as I listened to Diane talk. Almost everything she says is random thought now. She would whisper so she couldn't be heard by "them," so I had to put my head close to hear the words. We went for a walk around the facility, and her hip seemed to be bothering her a little today. The staff said she had been up almost all night walking the halls and got to sleep around 5:00 AM. She was so tired she dozed most of the time I was there.

10:45 AM Resident was pacing halls until about 5:00 AM. She appeared to sleep until 8:45. Resident was up in her room trying to get a shirt on for bottoms. She was assisted with dressing and seemed to get irritated when two staff were in the room so one left. Husband is here now and they are visiting and watching church on TV. No other concerns.

8:20 PM Resident refused to be assisted with all PM cares saying, "Get away from me." and "Yeah, right. You don't want to help me." Writer approached three times, and the resident refused to return to her room. Resident was suspicions of staff when she was trying to enter another resident's room. Resident did not believe staff could take her to her room. Resident made a fist and said get out of my way.

-- Monday, June 2, 2014 --

I arrived at the memory center at 9:15 AM this morning. Diane was covered up in bed with her day clothes on and sleeping. She was very groggy and didn't seem able to keep her eyes open. I couldn't make out what she was trying to say even with my ear up to her mouth. She had eaten breakfast and taken her meds. The drugs taken last night would have lasted only about four hours. I've seen her in this state several times this past week.

Courtney came by about 9:30 AM. This is the first time Courtney has seen Diane in this state. Neither of us felt it was drug-related since it was at least six hours since taking them. We agreed to just let her sleep as it is better than having her anxious and stressed. We'll keep her drugs as is until we can watch her a little more. We are both wondering about the cancer returning and maybe causing the tiredness. We'll use Tylenol as needed for hip/back pain.

Diane told me in her groggy way to "go play with my girlfriends." Courtney and I haven't heard that one before.

When Diane told me this, Courtney and I just looked at each other and smiled. It was one of those "funny dementia" incidents, but I wondered if Diane was becoming apathetic toward me. Thankfully, at this stage in the journey, I didn't feel hurt by such statements.

1:00 PM Resident was assisted with cares this morning but was very "weepy." Resident stated she was not aware until now just how sick she really is. Staff tried to reassure resident that she would be all right and would feel better after getting ready for the day and eating some breakfast. Resident agreed and ate everything for breakfast.

-- Tuesday, June 3, 2014 --

Diane was walking with a couple of residents when I arrived. She said she was very mad at me. I asked why and she said nobody ever told her about "these things." She meant being there at the memory center, moving, etc. She was tired and quite teary-eyed at my leaving today. It is still very hard to leave her like this.

2:17 PM At 2:00 PM this writer came upon resident pushing the B quad medication cart around the B quad. The staff working that quad was attempting to calmly redirect resident away from the medication cart. Resident was visibly and verbally upset. Resident stated, "Get away from me. You don't know nothing. My granddaughters are here somewhere." Staff then attempted to calmly speak with resident, but she started pushing the medication cart to the Alpha hallway. Resident then knocked all plastic water cups and medication cups off the medication cart. Staff

196

then called over the walkie talkies for assistance. Resident is now walking the hallways. This writer will contact hospice.

5:38 PM Resident is walking the hallways, seems calm. When staff approaches resident, resident states, "It's okay, you can go ahead and shoot me. If you don't your father will." Staff talked with resident trying to change the subject, but resident continued to talk about staff shooting her. Resident continued to walk around the halls.

7:55 PM Resident was talking to "a man" when I came in, but I could not understand what she was telling him. Then when I was performing her cares she seemed fine and was talking to me.

10:01 PM Resident is currently talking to someone as she is walking around the halls. Resident was in her room in her pajamas and ready for bed, but has not put on street clothes and thinks it is a Friday morning. When staff states the actual date and time resident states staff is lying.

I wonder how I would have handled situations like this if Diane were at home. I would be up all night, not being able to sleep. My concerns of overdosing her medications would likely cause me to postpone giving it to her, making things worse. I'm thankful Diane is at the memory care center where they watch her continuously.

-- Wednesday, June 4, 2014 --

Courtney is going back to school to become a physician's assistant (PA) and Diana, her replacement, was there today. Diana will be a good hospice nurse for Diane. She got Diane to take her medicine and let her take vitals. We are going to try another medicine to see if things can be made a little more comfortable for Diane. Nothing seems to work so far.

5:11 AM Resident appeared to have slept all night except for about a half hour when she allowed staff to change her into her pajamas and help lay her down in bed. At 5:45 AM resident was refusing to have staff help her get ready and was refusing to put pants on. Resident was yelling at staff to "Get the hell out of here!" Resident became violent towards staff.

8:28 AM Writer entered resident's room to give medication. Resident is sitting on the toilet in her room with the shower curtain pulled around her as if she is hiding. Writer asked resident if she could take her medication, resident stated, "Why would I want that?" Writer asked resident if she had any pain. Resident stated, "NO!" Writer asked resident if we could at least change her meds patch. Resident stated, "You could, but I am not going to let you." Writer will attempt again. Hospice came in today around 10:00 AM. Requested resident be given Lorazepam. Resident did allow hospice to assist her with her pills and patch. Will continue to monitor.

5:37 PM Resident has had the following medication changes: Lorazepam has been discontinued, and replaced with Haldol (haloperidol), one tablet twice daily, Haldol every six hours as needed for agitation.

-- Thursday, June 5, 2014 --

Both Norma and Cleo called to let me know they had visited Diane yesterday afternoon. They said she was doing pretty well. She could remember some things but not others. As they walked down the hall to the main entrance to check out, Cleo and Norma didn't know Diane was right behind them. Diane wanted to go out with them but couldn't, of course. Diane got a little teary-eyed, and so did Norma and Cleo. They felt so bad leaving her like that. Both got a little emotional telling me about it over the phone. I know exactly how they feel, as I've felt it many times.

Today Diane was in an ornery mood. She wouldn't eat breakfast or take her medicine. She wouldn't take it for me either. She went for a walk outside with me, but when we got back to the room she got very belligerent and snapped at whatever I tried to say to her.

9:56 AM Resident was assisted with cares earlier this morning. Resident rested in her chair and was offered assistance down to the dining room for breakfast but refused. Resident appeared to be having

198

hallucinations this morning. When staff asked if she wanted someone to bring her breakfast, resident said, "I'd rather die than eat something you poisoned." Resident was standing in front of her door making comments to anyone who walked by. Some of which were, "You're all a bunch of idiots here." When another resident passed by and told staff she needed to walk to work out her hip, Diane stated, "You better do more than walk to work it out because they don't do nothing for you here."

1:51 PM Resident refused her morning medication three times. Staff tried different times with different people and offered food and beverage with it. She still refused. Staff offered to walk her down to get some breakfast. She said, "No, that is not really what we're doing." Staff assured her that was all they would do and that staff could even bring it down to her room. Resident then grabbed staff's arm, twisting and yanking on it. Staff asked why she was doing that and told resident that it was hurting. Resident said she didn't care and that she was taking staff to the window to throw them out. Staff asked why she would do such a thing and asked to please let go because she was hurting the staff. Staff then reached for walkie-talkie, asking others for help. When staff had walkie in hand, resident then hit it to the floor saying, "You don't need help. I'll take care of this." Staff asked again to let go, and she did. Staff then walked away to give resident some space and asked if she would like to go back to her room or outside for a walk. She then hit staff in the back and refused to have anything to do with staff. Husband came in to visit. She seemed to calm down while he was here. After he left she sat in her room and ate lunch with no problems. Seems to be fine at this point in time.

It is reassuring to know that I was able to have some positive influence on Diane's behavior. She was in such a terrible mood when I got there this day. I felt that anything I did or said made no difference to her. Diane seemed to see me as someone she didn't want to have around. Attitudes and behavior changed minute by minute during these times.

8:31 PM Resident refused to come out for dinner or take her 5:00 PM medications for staff. Resident was hallucinating. Resident would slam the door while staff tried to talk to her. Staff let resident have alone time.

199

9:24 PM Resident has been pacing the halls and telling writer she is a liar. Resident stated, "Liar, liar, your pants are on fire." Resident continues to pace the halls mumbling under her breath.

-- Friday, June 6, 2014 --

Today is graduation day for our first grandson, Taylor.

Diane was not in a good mood today. She had refused breakfast and medication. Sue, the hospice spiritual counselor, stopped by but Diane was downright uncooperative and non-trusting of her. Sue said she would return another time. The massage therapist came in just before lunch and Diane was pretty relaxed when I left.

Taylor's graduation from high school was difficult to attend without Diane. She would have been so proud of Taylor, and Don and Heidi also. I don't think I took much away from the speeches or anything else during the ceremony. I just kept thinking of Diane in the memory care center and feeling quite depressed at her not being with us. I didn't mention Taylor's graduation when we were walking that morning because Diane often thought of Taylor as a small child. I didn't know how she would have reacted if I spoke the words "Taylor" and "graduation" in the same sentence.

-- Saturday, June 7, 2104 --

It rained hard all the way to the memory care center. I found Diane in one of the corner fireplace rooms with a white blanket on her lap. I sat down beside her until she opened her eyes. She wondered what I was doing there. She said the blanket was a baby, and she was babysitting. She had refused breakfast and her medicines. As we visited Diane seemed to be getting better. I got her to take her meds when it was administered with pudding.

10:06 PM Resident walked the halls most of the evening. When she talked with staff she thought it was her daughter's wedding, and she was missing it. Resident agreed to take a shower, as long as she wasn't going to miss out on the pictures, the meal and ceremony.

-- Sunday, June 8, 2014 --

When I arrived at the memory care center this morning, Diane was walking towards the office area where I signed in. She had finished breakfast and taken her medicine. She was in a much better state today. We went for a walk but our walks are getting shorter due to the problems Diane is having with her left hip. She limps significantly when she stands up after sitting a while. She was a little upset because she missed Chrissy's wedding. We finally agreed it must have been a dream.

-- Monday, June 9, 2014 --

Addy and I were signing in at the memory care center when one of the staff told me Diane was having a bad morning. Last night everyone thought she had gone to sleep, but when they checked on her early this morning they found her sleeping naked with a blanket on the bathroom floor. That must have been cold, but it didn't seem to bother her. She couldn't stand up until the staff got her into bed where she took her medicine. She was sleeping when we got to the room. I thought it would be better if Addy and I drove back to Chetek.

Hiding behind chairs, thinking someone was going to kill her, or becoming violent with staff members was one thing, but this incident really caused me pain. Diane sleeping on the cold tile floor with no clothes on?

This was a stunning indication that Diane's condition was progressing rapidly. For most of us, just having our bodies contact a cold tile floor would immediately cause us to get up. But, in Diane's case, there wasn't this tactile warning. Perhaps her mind told her she was in her childhood bed on a winter night when the cold wind was blowing and there was frost inside the bedroom window. I was also very concerned that she could not stand on her legs. This was one of those times when I wished I could be with her constantly.

7:39 AM Found resident on bathroom floor naked with only her comforter on her. Resident placed herself onto the floor. Staff found during her fifteen minute checks. When trying to get resident up off floor

201

she seemed to have trouble bearing weight on her legs. Writer has called hospice to update and waiting for a call back. Staff got resident dressed and placed back into bed, as she was freezing cold. Staff also noticed bruising on both of her shoulders. Hospice also ordered a wheelchair along with a tab alarm and pressure alarm. Also until further notice she will be a two-person assist and using the wheelchair.

8:28 AM Resident was walking halls until about 3 AM. Resident went into another resident's room and urinated all over the bathroom floor. Three staff members had to assist to get resident to her room. Resident was kicking and throwing her fist at staff.

4:47 PM Resident was in C dining room when she started to get upset. Staff was unable to get her to sit in wheelchair. She then threw a glass object, which shattered. Resident continued to walk unassisted down the hall, as she would not allow any staff to assist her. Hospice has been updated. Resident put in behavior charting. Hospice is sending a nurse out at this time.

5:16 PM Resident was in C living room and stood up from her chair. Resident's alarm was sounding, and I offered to help the resident sit down. The resident refused, stating that she did not want to sit down. I told the resident I would stand with her because it was not safe for her to stand alone. The resident then started to move the coffee table and tipped a small glass vase off the lower shelf. The vase broke and the resident was assisted out of the living room walking on her own.

5:56 PM Resident was lying in a bed in an unoccupied room when staff noticed that she looked ill. Writer tried to take her oxygen levels but resident refused. Writer asked one last time when resident punched writer on the left side of the face. Writer walked away and checked for bruising and found nothing wrong.

6:18 PM Hospice: The facility staff called to report a change in condition. When I arrived Diane was in bed. Staff reports they found her on the floor in the bathroom wrapped in a blanket. She did not appear to have fallen. No bruising or abrasions. She does have a new onset of lower leg edema and was unable to walk. She does not appear to have pain. She was up walking all night.

202

8:02 PM Hospice visit: Patient lying in bed upon arrival, easily roused, vitals within normal range. Patient had pain during stand to pivot transfer. Appears nerve pain to left leg is worsening. Nurse visits tomorrow morning to address additional concerns. Give haloperidol when needed to give decrease episodes of agitation/aggression behavior.

This 24-hour period was horrible for Diane and the staff. When I read the memory care notes for this early morning and evening I couldn't hold back my tears. Diane exhibited many different behaviors, all contrary to the Diane we knew. Lying naked on the bathroom floor, breaking glassware, striking a staff member, urinating in another resident's room, lying on a bed in an empty room--all deeply disturbing to me. Just one more example of what memory center caregivers encounter on a daily basis.

-- Tuesday, June 10, 2014 --

Diane was sleeping in her chair when I got there today. She slept the entire time I was with her. The hospice nurse checked her out. With the exception of a very slight temperature, all vitals were good. Diana, the hospice nurse, thinks there is a good possibility that Diane's cancer has metastasized to her brain. The kind of behaviors that Diane shows has been characteristic of "brain met."

I was so focused on Lewy Body Dementia with Parkinson's Disease that I had not considered the possibility of Diane's cancer spreading to her brain. I had a difficult time imagining how the brain might react to a combination of Lewy Body Dementia with Parkinson's Disease, Capgras Syndrome, *and* cancer. Diana, our hospice nurse has seen many patients in her career, and I highly respected her thinking and observations.

I sketched Diane as she slept in the chair today. It's a sad sketch:

Diane sleeping in her chair

5:47 AM Resident remains on 15-minute checks. Resident incontinent during shift and needs to be toileted every two hours. Resident pulled colostomy bag off during night. Staff put new one on.

5:53 PM Resident refused to take her evening medication. Resident stated, "I don't know what kind of poison you are giving me." I made attempts at 5, 5:15, and 5:45 PM. Resident was approached by staff and refused.

-- Wednesday, June 11, 2014 --

Diane was in bed half asleep when I arrived at 9:10 AM. She heard me come in and talk to one of the caretakers. She was very suspicious about me talking to a caretaker. I opened the blinds to get some light in the room, and that seemed to perk her up a bit. Diana came for her visit, and Diane was very pleasant to her. Her vitals were good. Diane said she had pain on the outside of "the butt." When I said she was a "pain in the butt" Diane laughed. She still takes small steps when going to the bathroom, so I think she still has pain in her legs and hip. The nurse had her take some pain killer which helped considerably. Diane laid down on the bed, and I felt around her stoma. There was a fist-size lump on her left side with a slightly smaller sphere attached to

204

it. The swelling continues into the area where her stoma is. I'm pretty sure we are dealing with the return of her cancer.

When I made the "pain in the butt" quip, Diane laughed, a genuine laugh, the first I had heard in a couple of months. She made it sound like her pain was on the exterior of her rectal area, which made me wonder if her spinal area nerves were being affected. She shuffles her feet in small steps to move forward. She also needed someone or something to hold on to while walking or she would lose her balance.

There was now Lewy Body Dementia with Parkinson's Disease, Capgras Syndrome, the possibility of cancer in her brain, and fast-spreading cancer surrounding her stoma. It was no wonder Diane was exhibiting such extreme behaviors.

7:02 PM Late Entry for 6/10/14. Resident refused all assistance. She did not come out of her room the whole shift. She stood up multiple times and transferred herself from her wheelchair to the chair in her room. When staff tried to help her or get her to sit down, she would refuse help. She would state, "Get out of here!" and "I don't need your help." Eventually resident sat down in the chair in her room and spent the remainder of the shift there.

-- Thursday, June 12, 2014 --

Diane was in her room sitting in her comfy chair when I arrived today a little after 10 AM. She was afraid of someone hearing us, so we talked quietly for a while. We went for a short walk around the inside of the building. It was a good morning for Diane.

I received two calls this evening from the care center. Diane had fallen. The caretakers had helped her to bed and thought all was fine, but on a 15-minute check, staff found her sitting on the floor with her back to the bed. They could see no injury, and Diane was in no pain. They called hospice and decided not to take her to the hospital.

5:17 AM Resident took sheets off her bed and refused to put them back on or let me change her clothes. Resident was very polite about refusing but stern.

205

5:23 PM Resident was very agitated and showed signs of anxiety. She kept trying to exit front door and living room door.

10:36 PM Resident was found in an unoccupied room holding her tab alarm. She would become agitated whenever staff tried to stop the alarm. Resident was found sitting on the floor with her back resting on the side of the bed. Range of motion was completed with no difficulties. Two staff assisted resident onto the bed. Resident said that she hit her head but is in no pain. There was no bruising or swelling on the head. On-call hospice, MD, and husband were all notified. Seventy-two hour vitals has been initiated, and she will continue to be on fifteen-minute checks. Due to being agitated and already in bed, tab alarm will be put in place to alert staff if she tries to get up on her own.

11:54 PM Upon opening the door, staff found resident snuggled on the floor at the foot of her bed, tab alarm disassembled and placed on her bed. Staff asked resident if she had fallen. Resident did not answer. Resident did state her butt hurt from being on floor. Staff assisted her up and back on her bed. Resident given morphine for pain in bottom.

-- Friday, June 13, 2014 --

I have Addy all day today. When we got to the care center, Diane was sitting in the large room in her wheelchair. She gave a tearful hug to Addy, and we visited for a while. Addy and I took her for a long wheelchair walk down the road past the construction areas. I think Diane enjoyed the ride.

12:34 PM Resident now has a four-wheeled walker that can be used at her discretion. Hospice asks that if she is using it unsafely it should be removed from her room and placed in storage. If she wants to use it and is using it safely, let her; however, don't push her to use it. If resident is very unsteady and having trouble bearing her own weight please use the wheelchair.

1:58 PM This RN approached resident, introduced herself. Resident stated, "I don't give a damn who you are." RN stated she had medication for her. Resident then swung at RN's hand, causing the medication to fall to the floor. RN asked staff to try again in half hour.

2:20 PM Resident took all AM medication. At 2:00 PM writer tried to give new dose of haloperidol and resident refused, telling me to get the hell out of here. She was not taking it and she didn't care. I was instructed by in-house RN to try again in half hour, and if refused again, try again at 3:00 PM. If resident still refused, destroy med and mark as refused.

-- Saturday, June 14, 2014 --

5:22 AM Resident took her 2 AM pill with no issues. Resident took off all of her clothes in the middle of the night and refused to let the staff help put her pajamas on. Resident has refused all cares throughout the night. Staff tried multiple times to help her. Resident got upset and asked where Jim was. Staff told her that he would be here in the morning. She instantly accused staff of "taking him out and getting him drunk to do God knows what." Staff tried to reassure her that he was not out at the bars. Resident then told staff to get out of her room.

The staff was very patient with Diane, even though she was usually belligerent. It is sad for me to read of her wanting to know where I was at 5 o'clock in the morning. I don't know how the "getting him drunk" got into her mind, as our use of alcohol was pretty sparse. I've never been drunk in my entire life and neither had Diane.

-- Tuesday, June 17, 2014 --

I arrived at Diane's at 9:30 AM and one of the caretakers met me saying Diane was really good today, very polite and cooperative. Her room was re-arranged with a hospital type bed that was raised in the up position. Diane and I chatted for a while, and I took her out for another walk in her wheelchair. I wonder if the increase in haloperidol made such a difference in Diane's brain.

I was surprised to see the new bed in Diane's room. It was another indication how fast things were moving. In a few short weeks Diane had become more violent, experienced pain in her bottom, had become more incontinent, and had severe problems with balance and walking. I didn't mention the different bed in her room, and she said nothing to me about it. Given the instances of Diane found sitting on the floor by the bed, it was a good to know that there would be bed side rails when needed.

-- Wednesday, June 18, 2014 --

Diane was pretty good today. I found her sitting in one of the living rooms by herself toward the back of the room. The conversation is very hard to hear, as she speaks so softly now. I have to have my ear very close to her mouth to hear what she is saying. The thoughts she expresses are very random and difficult to put together. Sometimes they make some sense, but most of the time there is no logical reasoning. We went for two walks around the inside square of the center, and Diane did quite well. Her backside pain is still there. It's very difficult for her to get out of chairs and stand up.

5:54 PM Resident took all medication well this evening. Resident appears to be confused as she has continually taken her bed apart. Staff has assisted her to remake bed several times.

8:08 PM Resident tended to toileting independently. Staff was unable to complete resident's cares due to being "out of it" or unwillingness to awaken. While completing 15-minute checks, resident was found sleeping in a chair in a housemate's bedroom. She was unwilling to wake up at this time. Two staff were able to transfer resident to wheelchair, and she stayed in it until transferred to the recliner in her own bedroom. Resident has not moved from this chair since.

-- Thursday, June 19, 2014 --

Diane was sleeping when I got there this morning. She woke up about a half hour after I arrived. As she tried to sit up on the bed she got a sharp pain in her lower back. I swung her legs over the bedside and lifted her up to a sitting position. The hospice nurse visited Diane also. All seems fine, physically.

This was the first time I had been with Diane while she experienced sharp pain in her lower back. I told her she could remain in bed, but she insisted on getting up. I remember feeling heightened mental stress and

208

internal aching when Diane was in pain like this, as if some of her pain was being transferred into my body.

9:36 PM Resident took all medication well this evening. Fifteen-minute checks were completed. She has continuously unmade her bed, spit fluid in room, thrown decks of cards around room, and tore up newspaper ads. Staff has cleaned up as needed.

Again I wondered how I would have handled things if Diane were at home with me. I imagined how difficult it would be to try to sleep, not knowing what to expect or worrying about something happening that might cause her injury. I often wondered what my own mental state would have been after weeks of sleepless nights.

-- Friday, June 20, 2014 --

I found Diane in her wheelchair in the living area near her room this morning. Later as we were on an outside walk, Diane fell asleep. When we got back to her room she immediately fell asleep. I felt she was hurting when she walked today. I think the haloperidol is making her sleepy, but it is still better than having her fearful of everything and being so stressed.

2:12 AM Resident was crawling around on the floor. When asked what she was doing, resident replied, "I am on my hands and knees scrubbing the floor. It's what I do." Staff assisted resident up. Resident was limping, grabbing at her leg complaining of pain. Will continue to monitor resident.

6:22 PM Resident wandered the halls both in her wheelchair and pushing her wheelchair. Resident's gait seemed unsteady. She said her "legs are broken."

-- Saturday, June 21, 2014 --

Diane was doing pretty well today, but, as usual now, quite sleepy. She is very relaxed and had taken morphine for leg pain. We went for a long walk around the block outside the center. She stayed awake almost to the end. Her conversation is very low in volume. I have to stop and put my ear next to her to hear what she is saying. She seems to be in pain when walking, but when I ask, she says there is no pain.

Diane still liked to go for wheelchair walks outside the facility, and we did that as often as weather would permit. It was just a few weeks prior that she walked *with* me around the entire large city block. Now, she couldn't walk and needed a wheelchair. I always tried to keep her awake by talking to her and pointing out things we were seeing. However, the times when she would nod off in the wheelchair were getting much more frequent. Her head would slowly tilt to the right or left, and her chin would lower toward her chest in what seemed to me to be an extremely uncomfortable position. She never complained of neck pain or shoulder pain, but it was painful for me to see.

-- Sunday, June 22, 2014 --

When I first came in the room Diane asked me if I was all right. She said I didn't look too good. She was very sleepy and didn't talk much. She slept all the time I was there.

After lunch Diane told me I should take my family and go; yet, she didn't want me to leave her in the lunchroom. That makes things very hard to take. I'm still afraid to stay too long on a daily basis for fear the Capgras Syndrome will return, and I'll be another Jim. I wonder if she knew me today.

It was another tearful drive back to Chetek. All this makes me feel helpless and deeply sad for Diane. I get emotional sitting here writing about things.

When Diane would ask about how I was feeling, it made me feel like she knew me and was concerned. As I helped her get dressed I began to realize the tremendous toll this disease was taking on her. I had to help her do numerous simple things we all take for granted like putting on shoes and socks, tying shoe laces, and buttoning her blouse.

I played banjo tonight, which is very therapeutic and gets my mind off Lewy Body Dementia.

7:53 PM Resident was assisted with evening cares. When staff went in to get resident for supper, she was standing in her room with her shirt off. The room was a complete mess. All the linens had been ripped off her bed, and she had taken all the stuff out of her drawers. When staff asked resident why she had done this she replied, "The judge gave the cops a search warrant." She spent most of the evening in the living room.

The stark difference in our lives is aptly demonstrated here. While I was home playing banjo to clear my head, Diane had been making a mess of her room, making it look like someone had ransacked the place looking for evidence at a crime scene.

-- Monday, June 23, 2014 --

I arrived at the memory center at 9:25 AM. Diane was on her back asleep. I sat by her until she woke up. I tried to help her sit up but the pain in her right side was so great she had to return to the reclining position. Diana, the hospice nurse, feels that Diane's pain is coming from tumor growth in the intestinal area and still thinks cancer has spread to the brain. Diane has been more calm but does sleep a lot. Diana said we can expect more sleepiness as time goes on.

When I returned around 3:00 PM, Diane was slowly walking while holding the handrail next to the hall wall. I don't think she knew me. When I asked her who I was she said, "16 years," or "17 years."

I was very concerned about Diane's pain. She was unable to tell us she was in pain, but her face and movements certainly showed it. The tumor growth in her abdominal area must have caused her side and leg pain. The thought of her cancer spreading to her brain, which was already being tampered with by Lewy Body Dementia, gave me deep sorrow. There was nothing that could be done: no cure, no way to put things in remission. I just prayed that Diane would be kept comfortable through this ordeal.

When I saw Diane walking down the hall holding on to the handrail and shuffling her feet to take little steps, I could hardly take it. I thought about turning around and leaving but didn't. It was late afternoon, and I usually spent time with her in the mornings. I think she thought I asked her how old I was rather than who I was. Her reply of "16 years" or "17 years" seemed funny. I thought of how wonderful it would be if we were both 16 or 17 years old again--back to being high school sweethearts-- but that was a long time ago.

-- Tuesday, June 24, 2014 --

I took Diane for an outside walk in her wheelchair. She was awake for most of the walk. When we were on our way back her brother Mel came and walked the rest of the way with us. She recognized him when he got close enough. She slept very soundly while Mel was there.

3:47 PM Resident was assisted back to her room after standing next to the living room wall with her eyes closed. Resident said that the "Diamond in the sky needs to come." Resident was offered haloperidol but refused by spitting the medication out multiple times. Resident also was offered morphine but refused to take it. Resident is currently in her bed and stated, "I just want to rest."

Diane's reference to the "diamond in the sky" is interesting to me. We had many conversations about near death experiences we read about over the years. Most referred to a bright light or a light at the end of a tunnel. Some referred to the bright light as God or Jesus. I wondered if she was trying to tell us that she wanted death to come, and the only way for her mind to express it was using a "diamond in the sky."

-- Wednesday, June 25, 2014 --

This morning Diane was sleeping in one of the recliners in the living room area. We couldn't have any conversations as she was extremely difficult to hear and understand. She was very sleepy, but, with her eyes closed, she began to remove her socks, put them back on again, put her shoes on, and shortly after remove them. She repeated this behavior over and over again. She would turn her socks inside out and try putting them on. She was so frustrated that she would start crying-- me too. She would roll up her pant legs like stockings. I asked her if she was having problems with her long stockings. She said a teary, "Yes." If I had a pair of long stockings I would have gotten them for

212

her. At 11:30 AM she just wanted me to go and leave her alone. One of the caretakers came in and got her into bed after giving her morphine for leg pain. She was sleeping when I left. It was depressing to see her in this state. I had a hard time leaving her today.

Changes I've observed in Diane within the past month, many in the last two weeks are as follows:

- *Inability to walk--just shuffles: Parkinson's*
- *More relaxed with increase in medicines*
- *Volume of speaking is very low*
- *Increased time spent sleeping*
- *Drooling when sleeping*
- *Nodding off at regular intervals*
- *Larger body movements and twitching during REM sleep*
- *Difficulty in sitting and standing*
- *Increased pain in the right leg and buttocks*
- *Inability to balance upon standing*
- *Increased difficulty swallowing, even liquids*
- *Slurring speech*

It is extremely depressing to visit each day and watch the progression of these diseases and then come home and try to get things off my mind by working in the shop, playing music, etc. I'm always wondering when I leave in the morning what kind of Diane, and what new behaviors, will I see. I get tears in my eyes often at bed time thinking of all Diane is going through. I miss her terribly.

4:58 AM Resident was trying to pull off the sheets of her bed, pulling at everything she could get her hands on during the night. Morphine was given.

8:48 AM Resident was assisted with all tasks this morning. Appears that resident pulled on hoses to air mattress causing tubing to break. Staff is aware and will be contacting hospice for replacement.

213

6:37 PM Writer gave resident her scheduled dose of morphine. Writer assisted resident into bed and turned on her bed alarm. Five minutes later, resident's bed alarm started going off. Writer went into her room and noticed she had torn off her blankets and was pulling up her pant legs and pulling her legs up to her chest. Writer sat with resident for five minutes to try to calm her. Writer called supervisor and was instructed to give morphine, which was not effective. Writer tried giving her something to drink, changed her clothes, and talked with her. Contacted supervisor who is going to contact hospice.

7:27 PM Spoke with hospice RN on-call in regards to increase in anxiousness (dressing/undressing, ripping things apart, constant rubbing of skin) since starting scheduled morphine. Contacted hospice and was told Diana would be visiting in the morning and to continue to monitor and give haloperidol if behaviors continue.

8:04 PM Resident was assisted with cares. After dinner she became very restless. She was fidgeting with her clothes, her underwear, her colostomy bag, her pillows, blankets, sheets, almost anything in her reach. She was restless and fidgeting wherever she was. She is currently in her wheelchair by the nurses' station reaching for things.

9:14 PM Resident was assisted back to bed at 8:30 PM. Resident has been sleeping since.

-- Thursday, June 26, 2014 --

Diane's eyes are seldom open now. I couldn't understand anything she was trying to say today. She would take her socks off and, in her mind, was at home mending socks. She would reach out for things, even with her eyes shut, and was searching for something with her feet.

I had a good talk with the hospice nurse. She feels that Diane's sleepiness is due to the Lewy Body and Parkinson's, and it is progressing very rapidly. There may also be signs of the cancer spreading to the liver. We will keep the morphine coming every few hours to keep her back pain in check.

As near as I could determine, Diane's mind was at her childhood home where she was mending socks. She would hold her sock in her hand and move her thumbs in tiny movements as if passing a needle and thread back and forth to mend a hole. She would put the sock down in her lap and then move her right foot forward and back, then side to side, as if she were searching for something with her foot. When she found nothing she would take her other sock off and repeat the whole sequence. The entire time she was going through this sequence she had her eyes closed as if she were sleepwalking.

-- Friday, June 27, 2014 --

I went to see Diane on Sunday morning. She was in her wheelchair, eyes closed, and head tilted back with her mouth open, sleeping. I sat down beside her and took her hand. She briefly opened her eyes. I think she knew I was there.

-- Saturday, June 28, 2014 --

10:24 AM Resident was assisted with shower and feeding during breakfast. Resident seemed to be in pain this morning and was given morphine. Since then resident has seemed very restless, trying to stand up, won't open eyes, and trying to take off clothing. Resident had one-on-one time with staff and was fed breakfast because resident would not open eyes.

-- Sunday, June 29, 2014 --

9:55 PM Resident was sitting in a recliner in A living room with her daughter next to her. Resident seemed restless and was fidgeting. Resident began crying and stated to her daughter that she was in pain. Morphine was given and seemed effective. Resident was assisted to the restroom and to her bed. Resident was not able to walk on her own. She was able to stand with one assist from staff. Resident refused to eat dinner and became physical twice. She hit one staff while they were assisting with toileting and punched another staff in the shoulder while he was assisting her change into her pajamas.

- Monday, June 30, 2014 --

At 9:25 this morning, Diane was lying in bed with her slacks on, and an unbuttoned pajama top covering her upper body. I helped her button the pajama top, but as soon as I got a button done, she would unbutton it. She tried to button a lower button. She put the fabric and the button through the buttonhole, pushing so hard she pulled the button itself off. She sat up and I helped a caretaker put the rest of her clothes on.

I put on Diane's shoes and socks and took her outside for a walk. She liked the warm breeze in her face. She just kept looking straight ahead during the entire walk. I now believe that Diane is not able to see. Diana the hospice nurse thinks the same thing. Here is why I believe this:

> *She doesn't look at the things she tries to pick up. She feels around trying to touch something.*

> *Her head remains looking straight forward, and she seems unable to focus on things around her.*

> *Her eyes seem normal when she looks toward me, but they don't make any eye contact.*

> *When we were outside, I put my face in front of her and asked if she could see me. She didn't reply.*

> *In the bathroom her hand has to be placed on the handrail before she will use it when turning to sit on the stool.*

> *If she sees anything, I think, "Is it an illusion in her brain?" She will ask about a person sitting on the bed or in a chair but there is nothing there except a jacket or bedspread. She might simply be seeing dark and light shapes.*

> *The hospice nurse raised her finger in front of Diane's eyes and asked if she could see. There was no reply.*

Diane will manipulate a sock, trying to turn it inside out, but never look toward the sock.

Sometimes she will put her foot out as if trying to touch or move something, but again never looking in the direction in which her foot is searching.

Tonight a little before 7:00 PM the memory care center called. During the evening meal, Diane picked up a butter knife and was trying to stab herself in the lower rib area. The caretakers caught her and got the knife away. Diane didn't hurt herself, and they got her to her room and into bed. I'm incredibly thankful Diane is there at the center.

I don't know what this event means. Does Diane know what she did? Is she trying to tell us something? Is there pain? Did she see the knife? It is difficult to imagine what Diane is going through. Sometimes I just want to cry my heart out for her!

4:56 AM Resident got very angry with staff when writer went in to give her meds. Resident was grabbing onto meds and staff and not letting go. She kept gripping tighter and tighter onto writer's hand. A dose of morphine helped her lay down and rest. Resident got up around 4:00 AM and was trying to get up and leave due to the "people" standing in the corner of her room. Staff laid her down, but she sat up and tried to walk right away. Resident then got angry with staff and was trying to grab at staff's face, shirt, wrist, and upper arms. Morphine was given due to the agitation.

5:40 PM Resident was attempting to stab herself with a butter knife at dinner. Staff was able to get the knife away from her. Hospice, and husband have all been contacted.

10:01 PM Gave resident a massage on back. Resident stated, "I like that. It feels good."

10:39 PM This writer was passing dinner plates and noticed that Diane had a butter knife and had the sharp end to her chest/stomach area and was attempting to stab herself. Writer asked what she was doing. Diane responded, "They told me to" and attempted to stab herself again. This

217

writer did get the knife away from resident. Supervisor was notified. Resident was kept within sight of staff while she was in the wheelchair.

This stabbing incident came late in the development of her dementia, at a time when we thought she couldn't see. Becoming violent toward herself was something new for Diane.

My first thoughts were of Diane trying to stab herself so things could "be over" as she often said. We had discussions during our time together about suicide, and both of us thought it was a very selfish act, that the person taking their own life wasn't thinking of the hurt it would cause loved ones and friends.

Diane's condition, put a completely different light on the issue of suicide.

The question for me is, if one has a terminal disease, if one is in deep, uncontrollable pain and has no control over brain function in a cognitive sense, is it better for all concerned to administer a life-terminating drug (with prior directives), or make a person as "comfortable as possible" while extending a dysfunctional, debilitating, and often humiliating life until the inevitable occurs? Death occurs either way. It becomes a question of time and "religious" ethics. There is no easy answer.

Losing the love of my life

-- Tuesday, July 1, 2014 --

Greg and I arrived at the memory center at 9:40 AM. Diane was in her wheelchair. We greeted her but were not sure she knew us. We tried to get some kind of response from Diane but got only partial phrases which neither of us could understand.

Diana and a social worker met with us at noon. They met with the hospice team at Mayo and recommended trying a slow-acting patch with Fentanyl pain reliever. This will give Diane constant pain relief and still allow the use of morphine. I agreed--anything to keep Diane as comfortable as possible.

Just as we were finishing with the hospice people, Diane said, in a rather playful manner, "OK, that's enough of this. You can go now, just go!"

5:37 AM Resident was in and out of her bed a lot tonight thinking she was pregnant.

4:06 PM Resident said she was very tired when she woke up and staff noticed she could barely keep her eyes open. Staff asked if she would like a shower to help start the day. She said yes. Staff assisted resident with her shower. Resident was being very cooperative but could still barely keep her eyes open. Resident used the wheelchair to go to all destinations and staff assisted with transfers. Staff assisted with walking using a gait belt, but she was very unsteady and preferred the wheelchair. Tab alarm on at all times in chair and pressure alarm in bed.

6:57 PM Hospice meeting due to change in condition. Increased pain not controlled with scheduled morphine. Decrease in vision--please cue patient when assisting with personal cares/feeding so she is not frightened.

9:22 PM Resident was stripping clothes, rubbing and scratching at her skin and trying to walk, but unstable doing so. Resident continued behavior even at music. Staff tried one-on-one with her, which seemed to help. Resident was unstable on her feet so staff kept resident in the wheelchair. Resident continues to try and stand up, setting off the alarm, but will stumble back when trying to stay upright. Resident kept her eyes closed all shift. Resident stated, "I feel so out of it," and shook her arms saying, "This crazy." Resident would yell at writer when trying to assist her. Resident is currently in bed occasionally setting off her bed alarm by getting up.

-- Wednesday, July 2, 2014 --

I went to see Diane today at 9:30 AM. I wheeled her into her room and played harmonica for almost an hour. When I finished she said she would like to lie down. She wasn't asleep yet and she said to me, "Have you talked to God?" I said, "I have, and every day I talk with Him." That was all she said and went to sleep.

I found out today that Diane's long-term care insurance only pays 60% of the cost for the stay in the memory care center because it's considered an assisted living facility not a certified nursing home. I called the insurance company, and they told me if I moved Diane to a state-certified nursing home they will pay the full amount. How cruel! By moving her, the cost would be close to $8,000 per month, $2,000 more than the $200 per day the current policy allows. So, I'll pay the $2,000 per month out of my pocket rather than move Diane, which all of us think would be very hard on her.

I have a total dislike for insurance companies because of the experiences I've had the last year. The absolute best care we have for Diane has been from hospice, which is covered by Medicare. Hospice has paid for most, if not everything. I still pay Diane's supplemental insurance premiums. What a deal for the insurance company!

The insurance company felt Diane might not get the individual attention at the memory care center she would get at a "certified nursing home." How would they know? They had never set foot in the facility Diane was in. The caretakers at the memory care center worked as hard as

220

those in a nursing home to give Diane the care she needed. In addition, Diane was under the care of a hospice team.

It's very clear that to the insurance company, a state certification paper is much more important than patient welfare. I've learned a lot about why our medical costs are so high. It is almost criminal that the insurance company still gets full supplemental premiums during the time Medicare hospice is paying for a patient's care.

I have told my children to be very careful about working with an insurance company for long-term care. It is my belief that insurance "providers" will do all they can with the policy language to avoid paying for needed care. It is definitely not about what a patient needs, it's about the company's bottom line. One needs to hire a lawyer to examine the fine print and legal language before signing a document of coverage, which adds more cost to being insured. Enough said!

-- Thursday, July 3, 2014 --

I'm sitting here at the memory care center beside Diane who is lying on the bed. She slips in and out of sleep. Diana, our hospice nurse, was just here to check on Diane. Diane's vitals were good with just a small irregularity in her heart rhythm. Diana and I talked about my reluctance to move Diane to a "nursing home" at this time. I felt Diane was used to the voices, people, and routines at the care center, and it would not be in her best interest to move to new surroundings. Diana agreed.

We got a $1,400 check from our long-term care insurance today. It is very welcome, since our emergency medical bank account was about depleted. It is still disappointing after paying 14 years of premiums, that there isn't more coverage. We have been through $25,000 in personal savings since March, when Diane entered the memory care center. If Diane were in the hospital with a physical illness, where costs are even higher, almost all costs would be covered. However, since she has dementia, it's a different story. It's just another reason we need more national discussion about mental health care. This should include discussions of the ethics of profiting from people's illness, physical or mental.

11:24 AM Residents paperwork has been updated due to significant change in condition.

8:42 PM Resident spent the night in the living room watching TV. She seemed to be in a decent mood as she was talking with staff and was not as jumpy and fidgety. She was a two-assist tonight, however. She tried to get out of her chair a few times but was easily redirected. She is currently in bed.

It is interesting Diane would be in the living room watching TV, since we were thinking she was unable to see. It is possible that she was seeing the scene changes and was fascinated by the phenomenon, or she might have been listening only. It is also possible that, at times, she could see well enough to watch TV. It's always difficult to know with this disease.

-- Friday, July 4, 2014 --

It's been a very emotional 4th of July for me. I miss Diane so much. After I got home from the care center, I just sat down in the patio and tearfully reflected on where we have been this past year. Last 4th of July, I hadn't totally lost Diane to Lewy Body Dementia with Parkinson's Disease. We could still enjoy each other and spend quality time together.

10:08 PM Resident was grabbing at her legs and had facial grimacing in pain. Writer asked resident if she was in pain. Resident stated, "Yes." Writer asked resident if she could tell writer where she was having pain, and resident stated, "No." Writer asked resident if she could rate the pain on a scale of 0 to 10. Resident stated, "It just hurts." Morphine was effective. Resident is currently resting in her bed.

-- Saturday, July 5, 2014 --

I arrived at the memory center at 9:30 AM. I found Diane slumped over in her wheelchair. She didn't look well at all. I wheeled her from the living room area to her room, and we sat for a while. I took her for a walk in her wheelchair around the care center and left for home after she went to lunch.

I called Don to fill him in on Diane's condition. I told him of her apparent loss of sight and the pain management we were using.

Norma, Diane's sister, also called, and I talked to her about how Diane was doing.

Diane in her room not feeling well

1:20 PM Resident was very agitated and starting taking her clothes off in the living room. I repeatedly put resident's clothes back on every five minutes. Resident was being combative and was punching writer in the stomach and squeezing my hands while trying to put her clothes back on. Writer then took resident to her room for privacy due to taking her clothes off and not keeping them on. I called the supervisor for help. The resident was trying to punch supervisor, but supervisor was able to give resident her scheduled medication. Five minutes later another staff went to talk with resident, and she was cooperating.

9:26 PM Staff took resident down to B living room tonight for a movie. She was a little restless tonight, and staff found her a couple different times with her shirt off.

-- Sunday, July 6, 2014 --

Diane had a rough night/morning. The staff said she had taken her clothes (shirt and bra) off in one of the living rooms. When they tried to help her get them back on she became violent, swinging at them and grabbing onto them, tightly digging her fingernails into them. They wheeled Diane into her room and let her calm down. She finally let them put her pullover shirt on but not her bra.

Diane's color looks much better today, and her face is much smoother. There seems to be much less wrinkling. She was really glad to "see" me today. She hugged me and was crying. She was complaining about a sore neck. I think it's from sitting slumped in the wheelchair. I brought her back from the living room area and helped her into bed so she could rest. She has been sleeping for two hours. She regularly has sleep activity: reaching for things, seeing people, and involuntary movement of her limbs. She actually looks better than I've seen her in several days. It also seems that she has to work a little harder to take deeper breaths while sleeping.

-- Monday, July 7, 2014 --

Today Diane admitted she was not seeing well. She made the comment that her eyesight is not good at her age, and she couldn't see the words on a picture she was imagining.

-- Thursday, July 8, 2014 --

I'm sitting with Diane in the living room area. I still can't make out what she is saying. She seems to be in and out of alertness. She drank some Ensure, but I still have to put the straw in her mouth.

I noticed out the window that Cleo and Norma were walking into the building. Diane was glad to hear her sisters' voices. We sat and talked for a long time. Diane was able to smile and laugh at some of the things we were saying. She was quite worried about getting a meal ready for everyone that was coming. We convinced Diane that we would take care of everything and she should relax.

11:20 AM Resident will need a re-weigh tomorrow morning due to weight loss of 4.2 lbs in one week. Resident did not eat much breakfast. Family came for visit today for most of the morning. Resident is very lethargic this morning.

-- Wednesday, July 9, 2014 --

12:14 PM Hospice visit: Slight yellow cast to skin, may increase. Both lower extremities have brown patches--this is OK. Decreased endurance/distant transfers. Do not ambulate, use wheelchair. Diana RN.

-- Friday, July 11, 2014 --

Diane didn't eat much for breakfast and got pretty restless. I found her in the activity center when I first arrived. They were reading the newspaper to everyone. Diane has no interest in the news, so I wheeled her back to her room. We are listening to old-time music. She is quite tired and sleeping with frequent body movement as if she were being startled in a hide-and-seek game. Her color is a little yellowish. She said a few words, but they are so soft and muffled that I couldn't understand them.

8:50 PM Resident was agitated at dinner time. Resident continued to try and stand up, remove her clothing and grab at everything on the dining room table. Staff tried one-on-one, pushing her around in her wheelchair, offering something to drink and toileting. All interventions were ineffective. Her scheduled morphine was given which was effective.

-- Sunday, July 13, 2014 --

1:36 PM At 1:00 PM resident was sitting in her wheelchair outside of the A medication room. Resident appeared to be agitated and hallucinating. This writer was preparing afternoon medication for resident. After administering, resident spit them out in her water cup. As this writer was documenting on computer, resident's alarm sounded. When this writer saw resident she was lying on her right side on the floor. Staff on A-quad and this writer performed range of motion with no complaints. Supervisor was notified as well as husband and hospice.

225

Resident complained of pain in her neck but requested to lay down in her bed. After laying down in bed resident had no more complaints of pain in neck. Resident is currently in her bed with her eyes closed.

9:36 PM Resident was assisted with all evening cares and checked every two hours for toileting. She spent most of the shift in the living room watching a movie and playing with the "busybox."

The "busybox" contained items residents could remove, look over, or generally "play" with. It is unclear what kind of activity Diane was doing when at the "busybox," but it must have kept her occupied for a short period of time. She must have been seeing well enough to pick up the items, examine them, and place them back in the box.

-- Monday, July 14, 2014 --

I arrived at the memory center a little after 9:00 AM. One of the caretakers said Diane had taken a fall in the early afternoon. The wheelchair moved from under her as she was trying to get up, and she fell. She is OK.

Diane was very alert this morning. Her head was held high, she was talking and able to recognize me as soon as I came into the living room area. She wanted to brush her teeth, so one of the caretakers helped her with that. As I was helping Diane out of the recliner to get into the wheelchair, I said, "I need a hug."

As I hugged her, she smiled and said, "You need more than a hug."

I said, "Watch it, we are in a public place." She smiled big.

This was one of those rare moments of joy. Having Diane recognize me as I entered the room gave me a much-needed boost. I could understand what she was saying, something that hadn't happened in quite some time. I will never forget that mischievous smile on her face when she told me I needed "more than a hug." I couldn't help but laugh. This was the last time Diane was in such an alert state.

5:11 AM Resident was checked every 15 minutes and assisted with toileting every two hours. Resident was up and down about every hour during the night. Resident was very polite and thankful every time staff went into help her.

1:51 PM Resident spit out medication that was crushed in applesauce. Resident has been very restless, unbuttoning shirt, attempting to stand up, bending over and pulling on her wheelchair peddles, throwing objects such as dominoes and Kleenex, striking out at staff, and having hallucinations. Resident appears to calm down while being wheeled around the facility, but when this writer attempts to chart, resident again exhibits these behaviors.

9:23 PM Resident was continually trying to stand up and became aggressive with staff. Morphine was given after three interventions were attempted. Staff spent one-on-one time with resident. She was given the opportunity to play with the "busybox," and resident was taken for a walk. These interventions were all ineffective so morphine was given, and it too was ineffective.

9:34 PM Resident was organizing "busybox" most of afternoon and after dinner. Resident did stand up from wheelchair three times for this writer. Redirected resident, and she sat down.

-- Tuesday, July 15, 2014 --

Greg and I went to see Diane this morning. We found her sleeping in bed. She had breakfast and ate with a little help but would drop off to sleep as she ate. We let her know we were there, but we couldn't understand what she was saying. It was something about going to the airport and parking cars.

Greg and I let Diane sleep for a while. The staff brought Diane a blanket that has long fringes on it for her to pull and manipulate. It was very nice of them, and Diane will like it and use it much.

I checked on Diane when Greg went to use the restroom. Her face was tense as if in pain, and she was crying. She told me she was having trouble breathing, and it hurt on her upper side. One of the caretakers

and I sat her up to clear the air passages. Her pulse was a little high but oxygen is OK.

I helped feed Diane today. She only ate a couple of bites of sweet potato and chocolate dessert. She had pain in her lower stomach when she tried to sit up. She said it was sharp pain.

Diane is talking to herself and taking her sock off. I really can't make out anything she is trying to say. She seems to be quieting down a little now. I think she is sleeping. It's 12:45 PM. She is sleeping with her knees raised up and one leg crossed over the other like sitting in a chair. Her right foot is moving, and she has pulled her other sock off. There is a lot of "playing out" going on as she moves her feet and hands.

Diane just sat up and is in pain. She still insists on sitting up in bed. She wants to sit in the chair, but just sitting is painful. We gave her medicine and some morphine for her lower back pain. After a few minutes her pain lessened. She wanted a blanket so I put one on her. She is quite sleepy but still moving her feet constantly.

"Pushy, Pushy, Pushy, Pushy, down by the station," she is singing to herself. "Clicky, Clicky, Clicky..." I don't know what the song is.

Diane had the melody right as she sang "down by the station"; however, I couldn't make out what song she was trying to sing using the word "clicky." The new blanket given to her by the staff never replaced pulling off her socks. I was very concerned that Diane's pain seemed to be almost everywhere in her body. All I wanted to do was make it better.

9:07 PM Resident had high anxiety today. Resident kept standing up; resident refused to sit down. Resident walked throughout the facility with this staff member with assistance. Resident refused to have assistance from staff member and tried swatting this staff member multiple times.

228

-- Wednesday, July 16, 2014 --

Diane is sleeping, covered by her bed spread. She is sleeping very soundly, interrupted briefly by a jerk of the body and a short snort. There is the constant 60-cycle drone of the air pump that is hanging at the foot of her bed. This all seems to be in direct contrast to the bright sunny green of the woods outside her window. Not even the sharp, loud, speaker on the portable radios outside her room wakes Diane. At least she seems relaxed, and there is no evidence of pain.

Our hospice nurse was here and checked on Diane. Diane said she still had pain in her tummy. We are going to increase morphine dosage to every two hours rather than four hours. The tumor that is visible in the lower stomach area is growing rapidly. The increased dosage of morphine will make Diane more sleepy but hopefully alleviate the pain. Our goal at this point is comfort.

10:38 AM Resident was crying this morning after breakfast. Staff asked her what was wrong, and resident stated she has missed her birthday. Staff took resident for a walk in her wheelchair. She calmed down and fell asleep. Staff assisted resident into bed. Resident is currently in the living room with her husband and her brother.

10:43 AM Increased abdominal mass size. Increased reports of pain in back and private parts. Husband reports grimaces more frequently. Increase morphine for pain. Pain may present as agitation. If needed give morphine and haloperidol--Diana, RN

-- Tuesday, July 17, 2014 --

Diane was in the lunchroom when I arrived this morning. She was sitting in her wheelchair, head bowed down. The caretaker said she ate very little. Diane hasn't spoken a word, even when I ask her something. She is very tired and sleepy. She seems to nod her head when I ask her a question about how she slept last night. Diane doesn't respond to my taking her hand; her arm is just limp. There is the usual body jerking motions every minute or so.

When Diane didn't respond by squeezing my hand or tightening her hold, I felt very empty, like losing something very precious. The limp arm seemed to signal that she was slowly fading away from me. It was a sorrowfully unpleasant feeling.

-- Friday, July 18, 2014 --

Diane was sitting by the nurses' medical cart this morning. I took her back to her room. The nurse brought in a dose of morphine and Ensure. She drank a few sips. It is very difficult for her to swallow now. It seems to take considerable effort to get the liquid down. There is much more body movement as she sleeps. One movement was very violent, and I grabbed her arms. She said she had fallen. I told her I had caught her. Diane's tumor in her lower stomach area is visibly larger. I would estimate it protrudes more than three inches outward and covers a third to half her stomach area.

The last photo of Diane in July

1:35 PM Resident became combative when trying to get vitals. Resident spent the morning with her husband and sisters who were visiting. Resident was taken for a stroll outside and is now in bed with eyes closed.

10:23 PM Morphine given at 4:09 PM due to verbal complaint of pain in her lower back and facial grimacing. Morphine was not effective. Morphine given at 5:09 PM due to verbal complaint of pain in her lower back, facial grimacing, crying and trying to stand up multiple times. Morphine was effective. Resident wanted to walk, so staff helped resident walk part way down the hall and back. Morphine given at 8:35 PM due to verbal complaint of pain, swinging at staff, accusing staff of hurting her, wanting to go home and facial grimacing. Morphine was effective. Resident received all scheduled medications this shift. Resident is resting at this time in bed. Resident states she is not in pain or uncomfortable.

-- Saturday, July 19, 2014 --

Diane is sitting in her wheelchair with a pillow helping to keep her head in a comfortable position. She is not very responsive. I wheeled her into the living room area and sat with her for a while. She got a dose of morphine and drank a little water. She is now in the recliner and has been sleeping ever since. It's about 11:00 AM. I've read the entire paper, every page, including the real estate supplement and am now writing this entry into my journal. I noticed that Diane's body movements during sleep have increased considerably.

I was planning to go to an RC fly in at Durand today, but I just couldn't make myself stay away from being with Diane. I wouldn't be thinking about flying my airplanes. At the same time I yearn for a few uninterrupted days to work on my Taylorcraft and do some yard work. I'm quite bushed after being with Diane and driving back to Chetek. No complaints, I would have it no other way.

-- Sunday, July 20, 2014 --

Chris called last evening. She and the kids had visited Diane, and Diane appeared to be seeing pretty well. She looked at Gwen and Reuben and spoke to them even when they weren't speaking to her. WOW!

Diane hadn't been able to see well for the past week or more; yet, she was seeing the grandchildren and talking with them. Another moment of joy! I was thankful Chris was able to see and experience this event. There seemed to be brief times when Diane's brain made the right connections. For some reason, on this day, at this particular time, her brain connected the images she was seeing with her beautiful grandchildren. Praise our Lord!

Last night after watching the movie **Titanic,** *I had a very deep feeling of missing Diane. It was so strong I couldn't help crying. I went into the bathroom to get a Kleenex and saw myself in the mirror. I think it's the first time I have ever witnessed myself in the act of crying. I didn't like what I saw and remember thinking, "This isn't a good time for a 'selfie.'" The crying continued until I got into bed. It felt good to get that out of my system--one of many times this happened.*

Now I am sitting with Diane in the living room area at the memory center. She is sitting in the recliner sleeping. Last night she was in a lot of pain. The staff called hospice and got permission to give Diane morphine every 15 minutes. She was crying with pain in her back, so it must have been very bad. She had a dose just before I got here. Even though Diane is very sleepy from the morphine, she is very relaxed and not in pain. For me, Diane's comfort is most important at this stage.

I brought my iPod with the little speaker and played **The Notes of Norway,** *her sister Norma's band, and then played* **The Sound of Music,** *another of Diane's favorites. Millie, one of the residents who wanders a lot, just sat down and helped herself to Diane's water jug. She too is falling asleep.*

11:00 AM Resident is currently in the living room sitting in the green recliner with her eyes closed and her husband by her side. Resident has had three episodes of behaviors so far this shift: restlessness at 10:00 AM when she first woke up. The second episode was at 12:00 PM. Staff tried to assist resident with needs and wants, tried to make resident more comfortable, and tried one-one-one with resident, none were successful. The third episode of behaviors was at 1:00 PM when she was punching and trying to claw staff. Staff tried to assist resident with needs or wants, massage resident's arms to let her know she is okay, and also stated, "I am only here to help." None were successful.

-- Monday, July 21, 2014 --

When I arrived at the care center today I received a call from the hospice nurse as I was signing in. She wanted to talk to me. I went to Diane's room, and the nurse informed me that Diane was on her last few hours. I called the kids, Cleo, Norma, and Mel.

Diane is having difficulty breathing, and we are bringing oxygen to make it more comfortable for her.

All the kids have come and Cleo, Norma and Russ, Norma's son.

Diane is getting triple doses of morphine now, and oxygen has made breathing much better. I keep moistening Diane's lips to keep them from getting terribly dry. Greg, Cleo, and Norma are singing hymns as I'm writing in this journal.

Once in awhile Diane takes a deep breath, making a rattling sound, then returns to small shallow breaths. Her body is very warm. "The Old Rugged Cross," "In The Garden"--beautiful old songs. I have tears in my eyes. I'm not certain if Diane can hear, but we are here for her. Precious moments indeed. "Have Thine Own Way Lord" is our song right now.

I'm thinking of no more pain for Diane.

Breaths seem very hard now. She seems to be grasping for air.

How fortunate I am to have family like this.

Diane, I lost you to Lewy Body Dementia on December 13, 2013, and now for the second time I'm losing you again. But this time I don't mind quite as much. I know where you will be, and we will be together again soon.

Son-in-law Mike just came in. He found more hymns to sing and played guitar as we sang. "Beautiful Savior"--the music helps mask the rattling sound as Diane breathes. "Just As I Am." Another two doses of morphine for Diane. Her temperature is 99.1 degrees. Cool towels are coming. Mel just got here. It's so wonderful to have her brother and two sisters here. There are a lot of tears in this room now.

Her hands are very warm. Breaths are about a second and a half apart and deep, almost gasping for air. "Will the Circle Be Unbroken." Just a Closer Walk With Thee." "I'll Fly Away."

It's almost 3:00 PM. Diane is resting well. Her breathing is still quite regular, and her chin rises slightly with each breath.

Greg is beside me holding his mother's hand and praying. I took his hand briefly also. I know this is going to hit me hard one of these hours, just as it did the other night.

Taylor came at 3:25 PM. I'm so glad to see him come. This is a hard thing for someone so young to see and experience.

It's 10:35 PM. All have gone home to rest except Chris and me. Diane is resting well, but the fluid buildup in her throat and mouth is continuing. We have a mattress on the floor for Chris, and I'll sleep in Diane's comfy chair.

It's been a long day, filled with many ups and downs emotionally. Lots of tears and much good music and conversation.

I've been keeping Diane's lips moist with water and draining fluid from her mouth as it collects.

I'll pick up on this journal later.

1:51 PM Discontinued medications--Diana, RN, Home Health Hospice

10:39 PM Resident was assisted with all PM cares and checked every two hours for toileting and repositioning. Resident's family has been with resident all shift and will spend the night with her. Resident had a lot of drool so Atropine was given and it was effective.

-- Tuesday, July 22, 2014 --

It's 2:20 AM, and I simply can't sleep. I was resting in Diane's comfy chair but couldn't get comfortable. I'm sitting beside Diane, resting my head on hers and whispering, "I love you," over and over again, telling her I will miss her, and that she should wait for me and I'll come.

I went back to Chetek this morning to get away for a while and do some errands. The most important thing was to take a shower and shave. That felt good!

Don, Greg, Heidi, Laurie, Mel, Chris, Mike, were all here today. It means a lot to have this kind of support. It's 8:00 PM and all have gone home for rest except for Greg and me. Chris is going to stay the night with me.

Diane's breathing and status is about the same. Her breaths are about four seconds apart. She hasn't had food or drink for two days.

Diane's brother Bill is on his way from Arizona.

Diane's brother Bill

9:16 AM Hospice visit: Patient continues imminently dying. Appears to be comfortable--oxygen increased. Stop vital sign monitoring unless family asks. Continue plan of care--Diana, RN.

-- Wednesday, July 23, 2014 --

It's 5:15 AM, and I've spent the night in Diane's room at the memory center. I haven't slept much in the last two nights, just a few short naps. Diane is the same, breathing at a rate of about four seconds between breaths. She still gasps in short inhalations of air. I gave her a long hug and told her I loved her but no external response. I checked on Chris, who is sleeping in the living room just outside this room. She is snuggled up on the couch. It's good to have her with me.

Yesterday the kids and I decided that we would like to have a traditional funeral followed sometime later, perhaps in October near Diane's birthday, with a brief ceremony at the cemetery in Northfield and a musical celebration of life at Norma and Cleo's church. Greg and I talked at length about the celebration last night.

Diane has had no food or drink since sometime on Sunday. She has lost the ability to swallow.

I went for a walk outside; it's a beautiful, cool, July morning. I gave Diane a face hug and told her I just came back from a walk, that I missed her company, and that I love her.

I checked on Chris in the living room area, and she was still asleep. That's good. She needs the rest. I moved the recliner from Diane's room, picked up some of the waste items, opened the window to get some fresh air in, and added two additional chairs for visiting. It already feels fresher in the room.

I took Greg's car to Chetek, got cleaned up and drove my car back to the memory care center.

Mel called and said he and Bill would be up tomorrow to visit Diane.

I set up Diane's comfy chair for the evening. I'm staying alone with Diane tonight--actually, that's not alone, is it? It's 9:00 PM. I'm tired but don't feel like sleeping, if that makes sense.

11:16 AM Per Hospice RN, Diana: "Continues imminent status. Good job with care you are giving resident and the support you are providing the family."

2:10 PM Resident has remained unresponsive and continues to sleep heavily. Resident was given droplets of water through sponge and has had family visiting all day. Resident was also repositioned every two hours.

9:45 PM Resident received morphine every hour and Lorazepam every four hours. Resident was repositioned every two hours and changed as needed for incontinence. Resident received a bed bath, new linen, and hospital gown. Lotion applied. Mouth swabbed and chap stick applied.

-- Thursday, July 24, 2014 --

It's 3:10 AM, and I just finished a stroll up and down the hall here at the memory center. Diane is resting well. Earlier this evening her hands were quite cold, as was her forehead. Now both are warm, and her temperature is close to normal. I've been able to take a couple of short power naps but nothing really sound. Diane's breathing is short and shallow but quite steady. I can't find a pulse anywhere, so it must be very weak. I can't hear a heartbeat even when I lay my head directly over her heart. All I sense is the movement of fluids in the lungs.

Diane has a little lamb beanie bag pet she got when she first arrived here. It is now on top of her chest between her arms and moves up and down with the rhythm of her breathing. I think of it as the Lamb of God, and that God is in full control of Diane's bodily functions. Everything is on His schedule.

It's 4:00 AM, and I just finished a small glass of orange juice and a mini bagel. I feel a little better and much more awake. In about two hours the sun will rise, and I'm going to get some fresh air. The

caretaker will be here shortly for Diane's 4 o'clock dosage of morphine. It's very quiet in the neighborhood tonight. I sat in Diane's comfy chair and fell asleep close to 4:30 AM.

I woke up at 7:00 AM and went for a walk outside and noticed Greg's car was in the parking lot. He woke up at 5 AM and couldn't go back to sleep, so he came down here.

Greg stayed with Diane as I went back to Chetek to take a break and shower up. I got back to the center at 10:45 AM.

Cleo, Norma, and Russ visited at 11:30 AM, and later in the afternoon, Mel and Bill arrived. We spent the rest of the afternoon together. There was lots of storytelling and laughter. It was so great to have them here with Diane and me.

Chris came over late in the afternoon and was able to spend time with everyone. She brought me a salad, and I ate for the first time today. Don and Heidi came over to spend some time with Diane and me this evening. They brought some muffins Becca made.

Diane is about the same. I fixed up the comfy chair, rearranged chairs in the room and settled down to try to get some sleep. The time is 10:00 PM.

-- Friday, July 25, 2014 --

It's 5:15 AM. I woke up after cat napping most of the night. Diane rested well during the night. Her breaths are now closer together and very shallow. The caretakers just gave her a dose of morphine. They also gave her a cleaning and adjusted her position in bed about 4:00 AM. I didn't hear them, so I must have been sleeping pretty well. I wonder if her system will continue all day today. I'm amazed that she has kept going this long. This will be the fifth day without food or drink. I'll try to get a little exercise with a walk near 6:00 AM.

It's 5:55 AM. I just finished taking a sunrise walk outside. It's cool, has rained slightly and looks like it will rain today. There was a break in the clouds in the east this morning which was beautiful. The clouds surrounding the break were dark, and those in the center of the break were a golden yellow, reflecting the rising sun.

It's 7:15 AM, and it's been raining. I'm sitting beside Diane. Her breathing is really shallow with short inhalations of air. Her fingers on both hands are dark blue, indicating the lack of circulation as her system proceeds to shut down. I continue to rub her arm and shoulder just to let her know I'm here with her.

Greg just walked in. It's exactly 8 AM. Diane has just finished her journey. She passed on very peacefully with slow, gently decreasing breaths. There is no more suffering--it's all peace and joy from this point on.

I recall the moment well: I was watching Diane as she lay there, her breathing barely visible. There was no motion, no sound, not even a visible swelling of lungs as she breathed. No gasp of air, no movement in any part of her body. There was a slight attempt at a swallow, and then everything stopped. Quiet, like drifting into a restful, peaceful place--no more drugs, no more pain, no more confusing thoughts, no more "other Jims."

I remember telling Greg, "It think this is it. Mom's journey is finished." I leaned over her and gave her a tight hug and kiss. The time Diane had wished for had come.

There weren't tears in my eyes, I just felt a loving relief that she would suffer no more. My grief had been continuous and deep since December 13th, 2013, when the Christmas tree was taken down. Greg came to her and gave her a hug and kiss, his eyes swollen with tears at saying goodbye to his mom.

We lingered quietly in the room for a few minutes, getting our thoughts together, then informed the care center personnel that Diane had passed away.

I called Chris, Don, and Mel. Chris and Don came over to be with us, and Mel spread the word to Diane's side of the family. Chris, Greg,

Don and I said our last goodbyes and waited for the hospice people to come.

The hospice nurse contacted the coroner and the funeral home. We decided to go over to Don's house and spend time there.

It was sad and difficult to say farewell to Diane, yet we all knew it was a blessing. She had been through so much suffering the last few weeks, and we felt a sense of gladness along with the sadness.

After phone calls to the church, funeral home, and friends, we started the process of funeral arrangements.

10:29 AM Resident passed at approximately 8:15 AM. Family was here by her side. Hospice arrived approximately 9:00 AM and coroner came at 10:00 AM. Body will be released to Burnham-Ours Funeral Home. All medications/narcotics were destroyed.

-- Saturday, July 26, 2014 --

It felt so good to sleep in a bed, particularly my own. There was a lot on my mind last night, everything from funeral arrangements to getting things moved from the memory care center. I woke up at 7:00 AM, got cleaned up and did some writing in this journal.

Our friend Mary called to see if I was home. She is dropping by for a visit. She brought some food for the freezer--bless her heart. She is such a good person. Tucker, her little dog, came too.

Greg had written a poem called "The Wait," which is very short but captures the feelings of dealing with illness like cancer and dementia. I suggested we combine the sketch I made of Diane with the poem, get a frame, and give it to the memory center. We went to Rice Lake to find a frame, get away, and "hang out" together.

Tomorrow we move Diane's things from the memory center, and we'll take the framed poem and drawing with us and present it to them.

The Wait
by Greg Adams

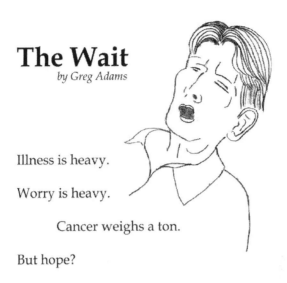

Illness is heavy.

Worry is heavy.

Cancer weighs a ton.

But hope?

Hope is...

Light.

"The Wait" by my son Greg

-- Sunday, July 27, 2014 --

We all gathered at the memory center in Chippewa Falls at 1:00 PM. I drove the pickup, and we loaded all of Diane's belongings and left the framed poem and sketch at the center.
We unloaded everything at the house in Chetek and relaxed for a while. Chris, Heidi, and Laurie went through Diane's clothes, sorting what goes to charities.

Moving Diane's belongings from the care center seemed strange, sort of like an automated machine where as soon as one part is made, the machine was ready for another, or like a resort owner getting cabins ready for the next round of guests. Diane was in the room a day ago then the next we were making it ready for another resident. I was thankful for Chris, Laurie, and Heidi going through Diane's clothes and other things. I think it would have been an extremely emotional task for me to do this.

-- Monday, July 28, 2014 --

It's a day to get prepared for the funeral. I washed the bed clothes, put away more of Diane's things, went to church to give the secretary some photos of Diane's home on the farm for use in the bulletin on Wednesday, and called the long-term care insurance to let them know of Diane's death.

I called Diane's drug plan to alert them of her death and also emailed the supplemental health plan because the wait was so long on the phone.

Jack and Connie arrived at 3:00 PM. We sat outside until the bugs got so bad we had to come back into the house. We solved a lot of the problems in the world, but as usual nobody was listening.

Having my brother Jack with me at this time was a gift. We had been through the death of our parents and grandparents, but this was the first time we had experienced the death of one of our spouses. Diane and I spent many hours with Jack and Connie, fishing and sitting around the campfire, but now we would be missing Diane. My thoughts this day often brought me back to that June day, a short year before, when Diane was unable to cast her bait. We shared memories of being with Diane and had our usual discussions of state and world politics.

My brother Jack solving "world problems" with me

-- Tuesday, July 29, 2014 --

We held the visitation at the funeral home just down the street from our house. There was a large crowd of people. Many friends and relatives visited and met our children and grandchildren. The flowers around the urn, arranged by Barb, Mel's wife, were absolutely beautiful. These, along with the many arrangements sent by friends, made a wonderful setting. Chris had created an outstanding display of photos chronicling Diane's life.

The visitation went well. I was quite worried about how I might handle things. I met everyone as they came into the funeral home, chatted with each person, pointed the guests to the large room where the family was, and told them family members had a nametag so visitors knew who they were talking to. The atmosphere in the funeral home was like a great family reunion. There were lots of stories, laughter, and shared memories.

The concerns I had of how I might handle things were unfounded. As a matter of fact, I very much enjoyed the experience and think Diane would have liked such a gathering.

I borrowed a technique from my graduate school learning communities to help ease the awkwardness of the visitation: nametags. Each of our family members had a nametag that included their relationship to Diane. It worked well.

-- Wednesday, July 30, 2014 --

Today is Diane's funeral. Jack and Connie visited with me in the morning, and we met the rest of the family at the church at 10:00 AM. The flowers and urn arrangement filled the entire front of the church sanctuary.

The service was wonderful. The family met with nieces and nephews for a prayer then proceeded to the pews while Mike was leading the congregation in "This is the day the Lord has made." I walked with Chris.

There were several times during the service when I almost lost it. But I was able to think about how fortunate I was to have Diane in my life for more than 50 years. Chris wrote a piece about Diane that was so precious it made me tear up. Pastor Guy did an excellent job with the sermon and incorporating some of Diane's favorite hymns. We played our instruments and closed the service with everyone singing "Do Lord."

Diane's wishes were to have a "happy" funeral. We did our best to make that wish come true; however, we also felt we had to honor the grieving process for everyone. The choice of hymns and the message was very "upbeat." But when Pastor read "Mom" by Chris (included below), my body swelled with emotion. When those of us playing instruments got up to play and sing "Do Lord" to close the service, I was able to regain composure.

At the close of the service, we invited everyone to Diane's musical celebration of life at a time to be announced later. The congregation retired to the basement for a lunch prepared by the women's circle groups. It was wonderful to share this day with family, friends, and acquaintances.

Mom
by Chris Rambo

It wasn't until I had children of my own that I really began to understand the depth of love that my mother had for me. There are times in the midst of parenting that I have moments of clarity as to how my mother felt as she raised Don, Greg, and me.

Once, as I was eating a salad, which no toddler likes, Gwenyth asked me if she could eat the croutons. Now, if it weren't for croutons, I wouldn't eat salads myself, so I was very annoyed. At that moment, I flashed back to the gazillion times that my mother let me eat every crouton off of her salad. How annoyed she must have been! But she never let it show. At the moment of my annoyance, I took a deep breath and let Gwenyth eat all the croutons off my salad. Thank you, Mom, for always giving me your croutons, and I promise to give them, with joy, to my children.

My mom didn't say much. It was her actions that spoke the most. Again, it's only after having children that I recognize her sacrifices of love brought her great joy.

Her actions, even up until the end of her life, taught me that Jesus is the Way, Truth, and Life. He will take care of us. Mom taught me to pray about everything. She taught me to sing--and that it's okay to make up the song as you go. She taught me that there is value in relationships, and a few very close friends are better than hundreds of acquaintances. Mom modeled what a loving and faithful wife was. She modeled patience and endurance. She modeled strength, beauty, and grace.

I will miss her more than words can say, but I praise God that she is in heaven with a new body and restored mind!

Moving on to celebrate Diane's life

-- Friday, August 1, 2014 --

I went to the EAA Air Show today along with Don, Taylor, and Taylor's girlfriend Jessica. War birds, homebuilt, light sport aircraft, the sound of round engines and jet afterburners--what more could one ask! I had a great time, and it really helped get me in a different frame of mind.

-- Saturday, August 2, 2014 --

I slept in after getting to bed at midnight last night. Even though I lost Diane months ago to Lewy Body Dementia with Parkinson's, I still have a deep sorrow and longing for her in my heart. It will take a long time to lose these feelings, if they ever go away. I just spent the day relaxing and took a nap in the afternoon.

-- Tuesday, August 5, 2014 --

I'm remembering the feeling I had the first few weeks of driving to the memory center to see Diane. That's the way I'm feeling now: getting used to something new and different, only this time it is reversed. This time it's getting used to normal daytime activities and tasks at home.

-- Wednesday, August 6, 2014 --

I had lunch with friends Barney and Roger in Rice Lake today. They were both very complimentary on Diane's service and particularly liked our family playing the last song. Many people said we should have played more songs.

-- Sunday, August 10, 2014 --

It's interesting how my mind is working regarding memories of Diane. While reflecting or relaxing, I am constantly thinking of our times together: wedding day, great times hiking, going out to eat, fun with the kids, and sitting together just being with each other (I miss that a lot). However, the memories of how Diane was since June of 2013, and particularly the past six months, sometimes haunt me. There is still a feeling of guilt for placing her in the memory care center. This guilt slowly dissipates as I think about the disease and how it manifested itself in Diane's behaviors, which required more care than I could possibly give. The images of Diane in the memory care center are difficult to keep from "popping up" in my mind.

I'm working through this grieving period by understanding the process as best I can, keeping active, and relying on my faith. Most importantly, Diane is in a place where all is made new--mind and body. That is totally reassuring for me.

The message at church today was on miracles. I must say that God has given us a miracle in the life of Diane and another in her death. I know how much Diane wanted the Lewy Body with Parkinson's and any cancers to be over sooner rather than lingering on and on. Thinking about the extended period of time Lewy Body often takes, and the same with cancer, it is a miracle that Diane could transition to her new life in the short time of four to eight months. The last four weeks went extremely fast. I'm continually grateful to have been there with her at the time of transition.

I went for a walk around 6:30 PM. I walked the long route that Diane and I always took. Even that walk made me fill with tears, remembering the talks we had so often.

-- Thursday, August 14, 2014 --

I had to spend time getting drug billing straightened out again today. The drug billing has been a real problem throughout this care period. I was being billed for everything hospice was already paying for. After informing hospice they called the drug company asking to re-bill them rather than me. Thanks to this great hospice program I've had someone to speak for me as I'm trying to navigate this nightmarish health system of ours.

-- Saturday, August 16, 2014 --

I took out my first journal book today from September of 2013 and read the first few pages. Upon reflecting, it's hard to remember how Diane was--that she had severe dementia. It seems like I was able to almost put myself in her world as I talked with her and was very comfortable with that.

She was becoming a different Diane. But she never lost the ability to love and be loved. We could always hug each other and hold on tight knowing we both felt our strong love for each other. It didn't matter that she couldn't make sense of things, that she saw people and things that weren't there, that she couldn't see, or couldn't walk. She was still <u>my Diane,</u> and my love for her was a great as ever.

-- Monday, August 18, 2014 --

Greg, Addy and I took some cookies down to the memory care center in Chippewa Falls for the staff. We also brought a thank you note along with Diane's obituary. They had also placed the framed poem and sketch that Greg and I did right near the office in the hallway that lead to Diane's room.

-- Wednesday, August 20, 2014 --

I took a hard look at my income and expenses today, and I'll be just fine. I can even spend some money on things I enjoy like RC model airplanes, music. I'll also be able to put enough back into the medical emergency fund to get it back up to reasonable amount. That makes me feel better. I'm going to be OK. Relief!

-- Saturday, August 23, 2014 --

On the way back from Rice Lake, just out of the blue, my mind was trying to recall the last words Diane and I spoke to each other. Early in the morning of July 25th, I leaned over Diane, put my head next to hers and said, "It's OK, Hon, all the kids are doing well, the grandkids are fine, and I'll be OK. I'll do fine too." I kissed her and told her, "I love you very much." At this point Diane couldn't reply. A few hours later she slowly breathed her last.

I honestly can't remember the last "real conversation" we had. It was probably sometime early last summer, a little less than a year ago. Diane knew at the time what was happening to her and knew things would only get worse. Shortly after that the Capgras Syndrome symptoms appeared, and often she didn't know which "Jim" I was; therefore, it is difficult to recall the last meaningful talk we had. It might have been one of our walks around our block, as we often had deep conversations then.

I miss her presence deeply, even when she was in the memory care center, and I never knew what she could or couldn't understand. I love her!

-- Wednesday, August 27, 2014 --

Last night at bedtime I was thinking about how terribly frightening it must have been for Diane to be taken to the memory care center, even though she wanted "out of here." This made for another tearful night. I remembered the time I brought Diane to the house before getting a haircut when I left her to get the mail and found her leaning against the hall doorway crying and telling me that she missed the house. It's heart-breaking to this day.

-- Friday, August 29, 2014 --

Today is our 55th class reunion in Black River Falls. It will be difficult without Diane. It's one of the many "firsts" I'll have to face: a class reunion without Diane. Then there will be Labor Day, Thanksgiving, Christmas, etc.

I missed having Diane by my side at the class reunion. Some of the classmates didn't know that Diane had passed away and were visibly shaken when they learned the news. It was difficult at times, but I always think of Diane as being with me and telling me to "move on."

-- Saturday, August 30, 2014 --

Jack and Connie were here for a visit, and the entire family came here for a meal. Everyone visited on the patio as I fixed chicken on the grill. The day was another "first": the first real family get-together since Diane died. It was a little emotional at times when I wished Diane were sitting beside me or working busily in the kitchen as she often did. But these thoughts are also comforting to me.

-- Friday, September 5, 2014 --

Cleo, Norma and I played music at their church until 11:30 AM. We picked out a couple of hymns as well as other "old" tunes to play at Diane's celebration of life.

On the way back I stopped at the Lake Hallie Memory Care Center. They had found a small wallet with photos and cards that Diane had, along with $29 in cash she had tucked in it. I made up this little purse for her so she would have a little cash and her "cards" when she needed them. There were pictures of the grandchildren, a picture of Diane and me and a picture of just me. Even these brought back tearful memories. I think it will take a very long time for these emotions to diminish.

-- Saturday, September 6, 2014 --

I spent most of the day at the Bluegrass Festival in Cameron. I have to admit that being there alone was rather difficult. Finding a place to sit alone was hard (I think it's the idea that Diane won't be sitting beside me again). We were together so much. Even though we didn't talk all the time, it is her presence that I miss. This lack of presence causes the <u>*deep*</u> *absence and longing in my mind.*

-- Sunday, September 14, 2014 --

At 3:30 PM I left for Eau Claire to have an evening meal with Chris, Mike and kids. There were several moments, as I watched little Gwen and Reuben play, that I had very watery eyes, wishing Diane were here to see these wonderful gifts.

-- Thursday, September 25, 2014 --

It's two months since Diane passed away. Sometimes I think things are getting a little better, and then there are times when it seems I'm right back to reliving the day and hour she died.

-- Friday, September 26, 2014 --

I've been reflecting a little today. There is no, "I'm glad that's over," or, "Diane wasn't the Diane we all knew," kind of thoughts. All my thoughts are of Diane when she was totally healthy, when we were experiencing life together. It's like forgetting about the details of a bad accident or traumatic injury. This is a very good thing because I get very sad when I remember seeing Diane slouched in a wheelchair, unable to walk, unable to talk, unable to swallow, and just wanting to sleep. Recalling those images causes me to become emotional in a negative way.

-- Thursday, October 2, 2014 --

My thoughts are returning to the last 18 months of Diane's life. The Lewy Body Dementia was incredibly difficult for the two of us. When I think about all the things Diane went through, the bizarre things she did, I feel much relief knowing there is no more of that. It's like her voice is telling me, "Jim, it's OK. Things are much better now."

My silent response is always, "But I miss you so much."

-- Saturday, October 4, 2014 --

Today is the day! We will have Diane's "happy day" at Northfield.

On arriving at the cemetery, we could see there were several cars in the parking lot. Greg and I met Pastor Guy and took the little white vault with Diane's remains and proceeded to our grave site. About halfway there, the couple who opened the grave told us we were in the wrong place--the grave was over by Norman and Thea Nelson's grave (Diane's parents). It turns out that they had been told to open the wrong gravesite!

251

After clearing up the confusion, we all walked to the Adams' gravesite. I placed the little vault on the ground in front of the gravestone, and we began the ceremony. I introduced Pastor Guy and explained the mix up in grave sites and told everyone that at least they had the right family. It all worked out fine and was sort of a "light" way to start the day.

It was very cold, windy, and wet, which made things pretty uncomfortable for all those attending. The ceremony was short and sweet.

Back at the church, I explained why we were doing this celebration and introduced each member of my family and Diane's family. Then everyone introduced themselves, and we began to play music. Little Gwenyth and Reuben just loved the dancing Limber Jacks.

Gwenyth helping me play the Limber Jack

Cleo, Mike, Mel, Me, Norma   Greg and me with the Limber Jacks

We got back to Chetek at 5:30 PM. I unloaded the car, ate a little dinner and "crashed" in the comfy chair. It was a wonderful day!

-- Sunday, October 5, 2014 --

I think yesterday brought a lot of closure for me concerning Diane's passing. The grave-side ceremony finalized things from that respect, and having that "happy" celebration that Diane wanted completed her wishes.

I'm absolutely positive that Diane would have loved the celebration. I can almost hear her say, "OK, it's time to move on, everyone." I'll be doing my best to do just that. However, she will be in my mind and with me all the way. Although I miss her deeply, I'll continuously cherish the wonderful memories we created together.

I see Diane's influence in my children and grandchildren. I also recognize the changes she made in my life. Her spirit is with me in the simple tasks we often completed together: cleaning the house, washing the clothes, raking the lawn, and shoveling snow. She is in my thoughts when cooking our favorite foods from her recipe box. There are vivid memories of Diane by my side when watching a movie, attending a concert, or going out to dinner. Her mothering skills are reflected in the way my children are rearing their children. Diane's likeness is visible in the faces of her siblings, and her voice resonates in the sound of their voices.

In these respects, Diane is still with me.

What an incredible life partner God gave me. Diane left the legacy of being a wonderful wife, mother, grandmother, and friend. Her gentle spirit serves as a model for our relations with others. Her care and sacrifice for our family will forever be treasured, and the memories she made with all of us will be passed to future generations of the Adams and Nelson families.

My encounter with Lewy Body Dementia with Parkinson's Disease was life-changing in numerous ways. In addition to losing the love of my life, this disease has made me much more aware of how fragile life is, that our lives can and do change in a relatively short time. It has taught introverted me that events occur in life for which you simply can't "do it alone." Situations are sometimes so demanding that without help from other people one can enter into a dark and depressing world.

Out of this maze of dementia and loss, I'm learning to redefine another "Jim"--an "other me"--and this time not one crafted from hallucinations and misfiring brain signals.

I am now another "Jim" that is slowly recovering from a long period of continuous grief, who appreciates family more than ever, who is learning to get out of his comfort zone more often, who is learning to live with the quietness of a single-person household, who highly values mental and physical health, and is more appreciative of what faith in God can do.

My prayer is that our local, state and national leadership will become more aware of the huge task we face serving and caring for an aging population and its associated mental health issues, that the trillions of dollars being "accumulated" by the world's extremely wealthy will be shared in finding a cure for dementia and other debilitating diseases, that the funds being spent on "fear of attack" can find their way instead to fund research to find a cure for brain-associated diseases, and that people of all faiths will learn to forgive and share a common love for all the "other me's" coexisting on this planet.

Epilogue
(Two years after Diane's death)

It is important to remember that all cases of Lewy Body Dementia are different. Everyone inflicted with this disease reacts in a different way, no two brains are alike. My hope is that sharing this personal experience will help others understand the complexities of caring for a person with Lewy Body Dementia.

My life is now filled with activities. There is constant contact with my children, grandchildren, and Diane's siblings. My friends are wonderful, my interests are varied, and my mind is constantly being challenged. I have a good attitude, sense of humor, and my health is excellent. There isn't much more to wish for.

Sometimes it is hard to believe good things can come from experiences like losing a loved one to a transformative disease like Lewy Body Dementia, but they do. Reflecting upon my encounter with this disease, one thought comes to mind: gratitude for the following:

God's message of love and hope. Without a constant prayer relationship with God my mind would have exploded at times. Taking the hurts, concerns, fears, and grief to Him, and knowing there is hope in the end, was refreshing relief to the constant stress of each day.

That God gave Diane and me 52 wonderful years together. Our love grew deeper as the years passed, and even more so during Diane's illness and at the end of her life journey. That deep love, strangely enough, lasts even after death.

Family, friends, and churches who made both of us feel well loved. It is difficult to imagine what we would have done without the help and support of our children, Diane's brothers and sisters, and close friends. Just knowing these people were thinking of us, praying for us, and there for us was an enormous help to my own mental and physical well-being. The visits by pastors were comforting, always giving us hope through God's word. There were also many times when church members brought food, flowers, and best wishes.

The Capgras Syndrome, causing Diane to see me as other Jims, seemed to disappear with limited visitation at the memory care center. Diane knew I was "her Jim" during the entire stay. She also knew who each family member was. Words cannot express how much that meant.

Our local Aging and Disability Resource Center and their Powerful Tools for Caregivers classes, which supplied us with countless caregiving techniques and offered excellent advice in caring for ourselves. Anyone in a caregiving role should take advantage of these classes.

The memory care center personnel. The young staff treated Diane with great respect and dignity. They have an extremely difficult task each day, caring for residents with dementia and physical issues. They have tremendous responsibility and should be more highly compensated for their service to our senior citizens.

The hospice care associated with our country's Medicare system. It's the way healthcare should work. The care given Diane during the last six months of her life was superb. Their follow up contact with me after Diane's death was greatly appreciated. Hospice personnel were our medical advocates who cared very much about what was happening to us.

The grieving process continues and will probably last a long time. It is, after all, a natural *process*. The absence of Diane's companionship and love causes periodic sadness and longing. Her loss made me realize that it is not so difficult for an introvert, like me, to be alone; what's difficult is being lonely. The words, "I did it, my Love!" come loudly out of my mouth after finishing a big task around the house or after entertaining a group of people.

Sometimes, when alone, I experience deep feelings of loss that result in weeping, and after passing, instill a sense of renewal. As my friend

Kathy, who lost her spouse to this disease, said so well, "Losing a spouse is so difficult because this is someone you are used to being with every day. Then suddenly, they are gone, and you have no one to share the little everyday things in life with."

People have asked me whether I'll get married again. In typical math teacher fashion, my answer is, "It's possible, but the probability is small." There are several reasons for this. First, I would not want a spouse to go through what I went through, if I were the person requiring the care. There is a fear, on my part, of repeating the heartbreaking experience of losing a spouse to Lewy Body Dementia or some other debilitating disease. Then there is the "starting over," getting to know new family members, their personalities, and traits. These are selfish reasons and may pass with time, but they are based on fears, anxieties, and experiences of the past several years. That being said, given time, it is possible to develop a best friend relationship with someone reasonably compatible. Having a close friend to do things with and confide in would be a great help in dealing with loneliness and lack of companionship.

My dreams and aspirations include being a good father to my children and a good grandfather to my grandchildren; continuing to play harmonica and banjo; working toward playing with and for others (particularly nursing homes); keeping my mind, hands, and body active through my hobbies; pursuing a life-long learning philosophy; and getting out of my comfort zone once in awhile. I do have a few "bucket list" items yet to check off, such as seeing a live rocket launch, visiting several National Parks and traveling to the northwestern United States. Finally, I will continue the endless task of moving our education system from one that is "system centered" to one that is "learner centered," a battle I've been fighting for more than three decades.

There are four things I pray for each day: good attitude, good health, good teaching, and good faith. As God grants these, my dreams and aspirations will be realized. Our marriage vows stated that the two of us shall become one. Diane and I were truly one. Now, half of that "one" is no longer physically with me, yet the memories we made together are part of my psyche. So, until I meet her again, I will spend my remaining time on this planet redefining myself, becoming an "Other Me."

About the Author

Jim Adams is a Wisconsin native, spending his early years in the small rural community of Hixton, Wisconsin. His life journey has taken him from flying model airplanes as a youngster, to assisting at NASA with one of man's greatest adventures: flying to the moon and back. After working twelve years as an aerospace engineer, Jim changed professions. He taught high school math, physics, computer science, aeronautics, astronomy, robotics, and several other courses. In retirement, he continues working with teachers in graduate programs and speaking to young people about aeronautics, space flight, and lifelong learning. Jim is a father to three children and grandfather to five grandchildren. He enjoys reading, nature photography, flying radio controlled airplanes, working with computers, playing harmonica, guitar, banjo, and being close to family and friends.

Made in the USA
Columbia, SC
15 October 2018